Restoring and
Refinishing
Furniture

We would like to thank Barnices Valentine for giving us his products to aid in the restoration process of the furniture in this book (www.valentine.es)

We would also like to thank Albert Fuentes, Haider Cano, Carole Montaigne, and Othilia Chaboche for their assistance

as well as the "Natura" shops (gear and materials)

Skyhorse Publishing books may be purchased in bulk at special discounts for sales promotion, corporate gifts, fund-raising, or educational purposes. Special editions can also be created to specifications. For details, contact the Special Sales Department, Skyhorse Publishing, 307 West 36th Street, 11th Floor, New York, NY 10018 or info@skyhorsepublishing.com.

Skyhorse® and Skyhorse Publishing® are registered trademarks of Skyhorse Publishing, Inc.®, a Delaware corporation.

Visit our website at www.skyhorsepublishing.com.

10 9 8 7 6 5 4 3 2 1

Library of Congress Cataloging-in-Publication Data

Manuel, Virginie.
[Vamos a recuperar muebles. English]
Restoring and refinishing furniture: an illustrated guide to revitalizing your home / Virginie Manuel.
pages cm
ISBN 978-1-63450-455-3 (paperback)—ISBN 978-1-63450-473-7 (ebook)
1. Furniture finishing. 2. Furniture—Repairing. I. Title.
TT199.4.M3613 2015
684.1'043—dc23
2015017386

Cover design by Rain Saukas
Cover photos by Bob Masters (www.bobmastersphotography.com) and Virginie Manuel (www.virginimanuel.com)

Print ISBN: 978-1-63450-455-3
Ebook ISBN: 978-1-63450-473-7

Printed in China

Restoring and Refinishing Furniture

An Illustrated Guide to Revitalizing Your Home

Virginie Manuel

Skyhorse Publishing

CONTENTS

Reduce, Reuse, Recycle

Sure, showing off something new is enjoyable. A cell phone, a pair of shoes, a car, a couch, a kitchen . . . We live in a consumer's society that causes us to accumulate tons of objects, gadgets, and other junk. But as soon as an item breaks, or even just "goes out of style," we stash it away or, even worse, discard it. Aggressive marketing campaigns and publicity make sure we are not tempted to repair or reuse something we already own. The slogan becomes: use, toss, and buy again.

An object's lifespan becomes shorter and shorter, purchases increase and, consequently, so does the waste generated by this endless pattern. More "advanced" societies have developed some noticeable linear production and consumption processes in which the excess of waste is the final result.

With this book, we would like to bring a little balance to these forces and promote the three famous Rs: Reduce consumption and its waste, Reuse (refinish) objects, and Recycle materials. These three words are the key to preserving the planet we live on.

Taking into consideration the need to adopt an individual behavior that is more respectful towards nature, the goal of this book is to show that it is very easy and cost effective to reuse and refinish used furniture that we have around the house. This way, we can break the damaging cycle of using and discarding by making small repairs and alterations inspired by imagination and creativity.

See for yourself: go to your local recycling center and look at the number of old computers, keyboards, freezers, washers, furniture, and other household items that pile up in the containers. Sure, some of them could be reused. In the case of furniture, many pieces could fulfill their purpose for many years to come with just a couple of paint touch-ups.

That is exactly what this book is about. Through a series of practical examples, we will show you, step by step, the restoration and surprising transformation of several pieces of furniture and other accessories.

Restoring a Piece of Furniture

Until recently, restoring furniture was considered to be typical of the lower social classes or eccentric idealists (like the first ecologists of the '60s), as well as fans of antiques. Nowadays, the stigma against restoring is slowly disappearing, paving the way for practices that show off aesthetic qualities and variations that new furniture simply no longer possess.

Furniture lends character and style to our nearest living spaces. As products of our daily lives, they can acquire their own personality and even feelings (a child's crib, Grandma's old sofa, Dad's desk . . .) that can affect us in more ways than we realize. Our ancestors, who passed their furniture down from generation to generation as a precious legacy, understood this. But current price reductions and the aggressive marketing campaigns of determined warehouses have started a new trend: "Redecorate your lives," they say. Using cheap, practical, and impressive designs, they tell us to buy new furniture whenever it strikes our fancy, seasonally, just like we see in the fashion world. There is a downside to this attitude. We are given the short-lived pleasure of change, briefly alleviating the heaviness of daily life. The materials, the place, the production, and method of commercialization all result in the object being a cheap product that has a short lifespan. This is the core throwaway attitude.

In contrast to this extravagant option, there is a more sustainable one based on the restoration of used furniture. Take note of its two fundamental aspects:

1. Restoration. This means returning a piece of furniture to its original state. Having to do with old and valuable furniture, restoration requires an expert hand well-versed in old or modern techniques, with a knowledge of and ability to use tools, products, and special finishes.

In this book we will tackle restoration in a superficial way in order to concentrate on a more routine and affordable method: restoration through

transformation, with a mindset of promoting ecological conscientiousness and developing inventive and useful skills.

2. Transformation, or the art of changing the shape, use, or appearance of a piece of furniture. As opposed to restoring, this is about reinterpreting a piece of furniture, using its qualities and defects to create a different piece, whether the change is formal (composition), utilitarian (with regards to function), or decorative (color and texture). The transformation, as well as being practical, allows for the use of imaginative resources that will give the piece of furniture its own unique personality.

Free Your Imagination

While restoration attempts to imbue the deteriorated object with its original splendor (as closely as possible), the transformation of furniture frees the imagination and makes use of creative abilities. Through structural or decorative transformation, the goal is to breathe new life into a piece, taking advantage of its qualities and peculiarities, and by playing with

forms and details that are no longer found in production.

This is also considered an act of remembrance, since we are opting to reuse and enjoy older shapes and structures. Ultimately, it is also fun considering that this type of restoration stimulates our imagination and allows us to freely express ourselves and experiment with each piece of furniture that falls in our hands. This way, we may restructure on older object into a modern one. We may even customize a modern piece of furniture so that it looks like a more original, unique, and special piece. It's all just a matter of creativity.

The things you can find . . .

One can find absolutely anything while searching for used furniture, although these smaller discoveries may have undesirable qualities, for which they were most likely tossed in the first place.

For example, we can find:

• **Furniture that has outlived its purpose.** For example, children's furnishings, storage file cabinets, card organizers, closet backs, barber chairs . . . pieces that are no longer used because of their owners' change in habits.

• **Degraded furniture.**
  • Because of the material: broken or deteriorated furniture.
  • Due to mistreatment: broken, wasted, or furniture that is falling apart, etc.
  • Because of superficial faults: scratches, ruptures, etc.

• **Outdated furniture.** It is old-fashioned and, as a result, hard to place alongside the rest of the decorations.

• **Useful disposable objects.** Packing and transportation boxes.

Where to Look

To begin with, it's worth taking a look through your home's storage rooms, garages, and attics. One can often find treasure disguised as furniture or objects from another era. Older generations usually do not subscribe to the modern mindset of disposal. Their houses can often be galleries full of memories, an ideal spot for a good "hunter" of used furniture. Surely, your grandfather won't hesitate to give you that old chest of drawers, or perhaps you can just "borrow" it and give it back later like new again. You can also look in:

- **Antique shops and restoration workshops.** These places are more specialized. They tend to sell furniture that has already been restored, but you can also buy unfinished or half finished furniture for interesting prices.

- **Flea markets.** Many cities in the world host weekly flea markets where one can find everything from luxurious antiques to cheap furnishings, to furniture in various states of disrepair.

- **Charitable entities.** Warehouses that sell recovered and restored furniture and other objects at very low prices. The profit is given to the workers (the furniture arrives via donations: an easy way to get rid of your junk). An international example would be the Emmaus Foundation, established in France in 1949.

- **Barter markets.** At these types of markets, you can exchange furniture for other furniture. There is no exchange of money and they are usually organized regularly by local or regional groups that you can find online.

- **Public auctions.** Organized by local governments with the content of homes seized by the law (as compensation), impossible inheritances, or due to abandonment by the owner.

- **Furniture collection spots.** Each city is in charge of organizing furniture collection events and it is best to ask them directly. They usually organize street pickup events or designate areas where you can drop your furniture off.

- **Secondhand ads.** These are a good option for finding furniture at interesting prices. The technology of the Internet and digital photography has greatly enabled this system.

There are also establishments where you may find objects for reuse as architectural components, doors, facings, restrooms and sinks, pillars, ledges, and, of course, furniture, boxes, trunks, mirrors, etc. These recovered elements usually come from old apartments that have been abandoned or remodeled, or even from antiquated factories or businesses whose office materials or other tools can be used for their original purpose or used in a whole new way. There are those who would use a smelting tub as a planter on their balcony and those who would make use of an old file cabinet to store clothes.

There are also shops that restore and sell ceramic flooring, mosaics, and clay pieces rescued from old construction sites. These stores give new life to objects or materials that are still useful and that often hold a certain historic, artistic, or traditional value.

Before Acquiring a Piece of Furniture

Start by performing a basic assessment to determine the difficulty of the project to thus be able to calculate the physical investment (hours of labor) and materials (cost of tools, paints, etc.). You might find that at first it's a little harder to approximate the cost of the project, but you'll soon gain experience and be able to much more accurately assess the total cost.

If you want to avoid rookie mistakes, start by working on cheaper pieces of furniture and move on to higher quality pieces as you pick up more experience.

General Assessment

This is about being able to appreciate or recognize the qualities of a piece of furniture and to imagine how it will look after its transformation. The aspects that come into play here are style, function, and the size of the space that the piece will eventually have to fit into.

Before acquiring a piece of furniture, it is advisable to observe and ask yourself a series of questions:

At the functional level

- Do we really need a piece of furniture that does this?
- Can we adapt the piece to fulfill a more useful need?
- Will it be practical to use it in the manner we are thinking? For example, a fantastic file cabinet that won't be able to open all the way because of a lack of space . . .

At the aesthetic level

It is important to visualize the piece of furniture we are about to restore to make sure it will go with the space we are planning to put it in. For example, a pop seventies-style piece of furniture will most likely not go well in a rustic-style house. Although many dare to mix different styles, it is advisable, at the beginning, to avoid attempting to force together greatly contracting styles. In a neutral home, we run into fewer stylistic problems since the special object is allowed to stand out. Both modern furniture as well as old will have their spot and the opportunity to influence the space, even if it is in contrasting ways.

At the spatial level

It may seem obvious, but it is actually complicated trying to visualize whether a piece of furniture will fit in the space we have planned for it. How many times have we arrived home with a new piece of furniture only to find, to our dismay, that is doesn't fit where we had planned to show it off?

A piece of furniture can be neither too bulky (taking up too much space) or too small (it becomes lost among everything else).

These three considerations are essential for the piece to fulfill its new function and avoid being once again abandoned in the attic.

Assessing Damages and Alterations

When acquiring a piece of used furniture, it is key to analyze its condition to be able to calculate the amount of work it will take to restore it. To do this, we must always do an in-depth examination and pay special attention to the following details:

- Strength and stability, checking the structure (fittings, feet, rungs, etc.)
- Surface (paint and varnish)
- Verifying that all mechanisms are working (collapsible furniture, drawers, etc.)
- Take inventory of small pieces (iron fittings, frames, etc.)

Once we've examined the furniture to be restored, it's important to learn to recognize the causes of its initial deterioration. It would be pointless to fill wood-worm holes, paint a rotten wooden table, or apply an anti-rust coating if we haven't discovered the cause of these problems in the first place. Remember that each type of material has its own intrinsic properties as well as its own variations.

Used Furniture's Enemies

Biological Agents

Fungi and xylophagous insects in the wood (such as termites or woodworm).

Fungi first show up as small blemishes on the surface of affected wood. The fungus will cause the wood to break down, splitting apart the fibers and forcing the material to soften, fall apart, and lose all consistency. In humid environments, the rot can spread quickly.

Xylophagous insects and fungi can affect the surface as well as the structure of a piece of furniture, spreading at a breakneck pace. So, at the very first sign, don't hesitate to isolate the affected piece from the rest of your furniture.

It is important to adequately protect and preserve the piece of furniture by adapting it to its surroundings. Because of this, it is advisable to place it in a well-ventilated and dry spot. A typical case of furniture infested with fungi happens when it has been left for a long time in some humid corner of the house (a patio, the garage, a garden, etc.). A fungus attack begins when the humidity of the wood rises above twenty percent (twenty-five percent for more resistant types of wood). An increased percentage of humidity can be caused by proximity to stagnant water, condensed water, capillary moisture, porosity, or rupturing of water lines.

Another great enemy of used furniture is **xylophagous insects**, small bugs that can leave wood looking like Gruyère cheese. It is a destructive plague that can spread quite quickly, especially during warmer periods. The most common species in our latitude are woodworm and termites.

In most cases, parasites lay eggs in the outer layers and cracks of the wood. Afterwards, the larvae feed on the starch and cellulose, forming winding tunnels that end up destroying the firmness of the wood.

The most important and fundamental way of controlling wood-eating fungi is to eliminate the sources

of moisture that spurred its appearance, since by simply treating the wood with chemicals, you cannot be sure that it won't just become infected again.

Woodworms are one of the most common xylophagous insects in furniture. They can be readily identified by the holes (about 1 mm, or 3/64 in. in diameter) left by the larvae that hatch inside the wood and burrow their way out. The sawdust residue around the hole is a sure sign of recent activity and an indication that you must immediately start eliminating the insect to protect the piece of furniture.

The types of wood that are more susceptible to woodworm are neither very young nor very old, being just dry enough to enable easy excavation.

Termites live in colonies and grow in darkness inside the wood, leaving no clues on the outside. They prefer thicker wood, such as rafters and the trunks of older trees. They usually burrow very aggressively and it is often too late once the infestation is spotted. The only option is usually to get rid of the piece and try to eliminate the infestation completely to avoid it spreading throughout its surroundings.

One of the most important steps in preventing the appearance of xylophagous insects is to avoid damaging the wood (cracks, fissures, holes, etc.) in order to prevent them from laying their eggs inside it. It is also important to protect the wood by using sealants and finishes that create a physical barrier: paint, wax, varnish, and shellac.

Environmental Factors

There are mainly three ways in which external and weather-related factors damage wood:

- Changes in humidity that cause expansion followed by rotting of the wood and its derivatives, such as plywood, composite, and pressed wood. The last two are usually covered with a layer of melamine that, if damaged, can leave the wood unprotected

and accelerate its decline. Humidity in the air is also responsible for the corrosion of metals (via oxidation) and plastics.

- Salts. When exposed to moisture, they can worsen the corrosion of furniture. It is advisable to protect your furniture from this environmental agent, especially if you are near the ocean.

- Sunlight. Causes discoloration of wood and splitting of finishes.

Mechanical Damage

Any damage caused by blows, excess weight, inappropriate or sharp movements, breaks, cracks, etc.

- Previous restorative work done poorly, using inadequate material or low quality labor: bad welding or gluing, minor household repairs and spot-fixing, etc.

- Chemical damage: burns, stains, etc.

The Three Stages of Restoration

1. Refurbishing

2. Small and Original Changes

3. The Best Finish

Safety and Useful Tips

The work space

Upon starting a do-it-yourself project or decoration, it's important to have a comfortable, practical, and enjoyable work space that will speed up and improve results.

- **A safe space adapted to the needs of the project.** Whenever possible, it is suggested to work in a large space to be able to move freely around the piece of furniture and to avoid having to move it during the project. An outside area, such as a balcony, garden, or porch is ideal so long as atmospheric conditions prove favorable. Mind you, during the drying phase, it's important to protect the furniture from humidity as well as sunlight to avoid damaging the unfinished project. We also advise protecting the ground and your surroundings with cardboard and plastic to avoid damage and

cleanup costs after the project. Try not to work too close to the kitchen or pantry, and work far away from heat sources (high temperatures can dry out the wood, and fire can react unfavorably with any vapors that might be produced by the use of chemicals). A work bench or a well-protected table will prove useful when stripping, restoring, or painting a piece of furniture by allowing you to work at a comfortable height. It would also be useful for cutting and sawing by providing a firm surface that won't move when you need to apply force to the piece of furniture.

- **Organizing your tools and materials.** Efficient organization will speed up your work by helping you avoid pointless side trips or wastes of time. A special note here about toxic products: they should always be properly sealed and stored after use in a safe spot far out of reach of curious children (preferably in a locked closet or cabinet away from any heat source). When storing many products together, you should clearly label each one in order to avoid potential accidents and waste so that you do not have to repurchase them.

- **Ventilation.** When using toxic products during restoration projects, it is always wise to work outdoors. If this is not possible or there is not enough space, try to open all windows and wear protective face masks. If working outdoors, remember that wind and dust are not your friends, especially during projects involving paint and varnish.

- **Lighting.** Having good lighting will allow you to work comfortably and precisely. Whenever possible, try to work with natural lighting. Otherwise, we suggest using fluorescent lighting overall and stronger lights for areas with machinery and where more precise work is done.

- **Temperature.** We advise working in temperate areas (neither too cold nor too hot) as much for your own comfort as to ensure the right application of any products you are using (applying, drying, etc.).

- **Electrical tools.** It is important to use extreme caution when handling electrical tools. Always disconnect them when they are not in use and arrange any cables so that you won't accidentally step on them or squish them (for example, with the foot of a piece of furniture) and avoid bringing them into contact with liquids.

- **Waste.** It helps to separate different types of waste and arrange them in small bags to avoid any rips or tears caused by excess weight and so that it is easier to move. On one  side we can put our leftover wood, removing or sinking the nails, as well as our leftover rusted metal. In a different, sealable bag, we can put our chemical waste, once dry, as well as dust, stripped paint, and pieces of plastic.

Organizing the work

- It is best to plan your work in such a way that you can organize all our tools, products, and safety materials needed to complete each of the tasks. This way you can arrange your space and tools to avoid any unwanted disturbances.

- Before getting to work, you want to plan the purchase of any products and tools that you will need so that we can avoid having to stop working halfway through the project.

- You should also be sure to be cleaning and organizing your work space as you are working. This way, you are keeping what you are doing fresh in your mind and can continue making plans for what lies ahead. For example, you must clean your work space between stripping and sanding.

- Avoid doing any kind of work that will create dust when you are applying a finish. For example, sanding and drying varnish cannot be done at the same time, since the dust could damage the smooth surface of the varnish.

Dismantling Furniture

Before doing anything else, remember that it's much easier to work on the individual parts of a piece of furniture, especially when stripping or painting. To begin with, remove any drawers and loose parts so you don't have to worry about them while you work.

Then remove any iron fittings you find on the furniture. Now you can begin unscrewing any knobs, hinges, or handles, being careful not to break them. Sometimes you'll find an excessive amount of rust on the screws and this step can become more complicated than it first seemed. It's important not to force any anchoring parts, as you could break or ruin the supports or any other irreplaceable part. A good dose of lubricating oil can make this easier. It's important to apply the oil directly onto the nail or screw and to avoid getting any on the surrounding areas as the grease can make the painting process more difficult.

If the piece of furniture is very old, it's possible that the hinges might have been nailed in. Plus, if the nails are round-headed, the dismantling process could become even more complicated. If this is the case, we recommend lifting the hinge by slipping a trowel or thin piece of metal between the wood and the hinge that will serve to protect the wood underneath. Next, use a screwdriver as a lever between the hinge and the trowel.

Once you've lifted the nails a bit, you can pull them out with the help of a pair of tongs or pliers, trying to preserve the nails as much as possible.

What do I need?
▶ Screwdrivers and nut drivers
▶ Trowel
▶ Pliers
▶ Tongs
▶ Hammer
▶ An old, dull chisel
▶ Lubricating oil

Cleaning Time

What do I need?

▸ **Bristle brush.** Plant-based and with tough bristles that will let you rub the surface of a piece of furniture without scratching it. Also used for cleaning and removing dust and filth or blotches with the help of some kind of detergent.

▸ **Soap.** Marseille soap for degreasing or removing blotches. Used on finished surfaces (painted or varnished) and diluted with cold or lukewarm water.

If the surface of the wood is untreated, you should not water down the mixture too much because it will take longer to dry and it could open the grain. To avoid this, try sanding very lightly to close the grain back up.

▸ **Varnish cleaner.** This is a mixture of neutral soap, water, ammonia, and wax flakes, used often for cleaning varnished surfaces.

▸ **Vinegar.** Used for removing grease from all types of surfaces, mixed with cold or lukewarm water. When undiluted and soaked into a soft rag, it is used for shining metal.

▸ **Ammonia.** Powerful grease remover, usually diluted with water and/or other ingredients (for example, varnish cleaner). Due to its high toxicity, caution is advised.

▸ **Acetone.** Power solvent used for removing blotches and tingeing plastic. Do not inhale.

▸ **Cotton rags.** They don't leave behind threads or fuzz, especially if they are well-used and have been washed many times. Great for creating rag balls that will be use to apply sealer or wax, as well as for cleaning leftover dust and polishing. Can be made with very old, very clean rags.

▸ **Alcohol.** The most innocuous of the cleaning products, used for cleaning delicate wood and dissolving varnish.

▸ **Turpentine and solvents.** Used for removing and cleaning paint, varnish, and wax.

▸ **Scouring pad.** This is a wad of fibers, usually plant-based, used for rubbing without scratching.

▸ **Metal scouring pad.** Wad of metal fibers used for scratching, rubbing, and polishing (fine pads). There are several degrees of thickness.

▸ **Oxalic acid.** Used for making whitening solutions used for eliminating blotches from iron and wood.

▸ **Trowel.** Used for getting rid of stuck junk, paint, etc.

▸ **Gloves.** Best when made of thick plastic, and resistant to contact with chemical products, ensuring that your skin is well protected.

▸ **Sponges.** Ideal for cleaning the surfaces of the piece of furniture being treated.

Before applying a decorative finish, especially when dealing with refurbished furniture, it's important to thoroughly clean it to remove any grease stains, dirt, fluff, stuck garbage (gum, stickers, plaster, etc.), and any impurities that may have accumulated with use over time on the surface or corners of the furniture. Remember that a deep clean can change the appearance of a piece of furniture and reveal its aesthetic qualities as well as important faults or defects that, until now, may have been hidden or disguised (for example, woodworm infestation, rot, stains, and discoloration).

Before using any chemical products, be sure to research their specifications, usage warnings, and compatibility with the material of the piece of furniture, be it wood, plastic, iron, or any other material.

How to remove stains and clean a surface

- **Stains in general.** With the aid of a fine steel scouring pad, rub the surface using a furniture cleaner.

- **Grease and oil.** Greasy or oily stains on porous surfaces such as wood must be cleaned as soon as they appear. If you allow time to pass, the stain will sink into the wood and it will be practically impossible to completely clean, unless the wood is particularly sturdy and you sand it deeply. Talcum powder or a stain removing agent will be enough to immediately absorb the stain.

- **Iron oxide and clearing the wood.** Rub with a piece of cotton soaked in hydrogen peroxide and then rinse the wood with lukewarm water and ammonia.

  - You can also try using a solution of oxalic acid. In a glass container filled with lukewarm water, add the oxalic acid crystals bit by bit, mixing until the solution is saturated (the crystals stop dissolving). Let the solution sit for ten minutes and then brush it on with a synthetic brush.

- **Resin stains.** Scour with a scraper and then use solvents.

Be careful when using cleaning products

The products and chemical agents used for cleaning furniture tend to be quite toxic, as well as irritating to the skin and eyes. It is not a good idea to mix them with other similar products as they could let off very toxic gases. We suggest you use gloves and safety glasses when you are mixing and using these products. It's also a good idea to try them out on some other surface beforehand just to gauge the possible damage they could do to your furniture.

Handy tips

▶ **Moisture spots or cigarette burns.** Rub along the grain using a mixture of cigarette ash and olive oil. Next, clean and polish using a dry rag.

▶ **Blotches on unvarnished or un-waxed pine.** Apply lighter fluid and then turpentine and raw linseed oil in equal parts.

▶ **Leftover wax.** Heat the wax and rub it off with a rag dampened with turpentine.

▶ **Ink blots.** Use blotting paper and denatured alcohol. If there is still ink, the only solution will be to carefully sand and cover.

▶ **Faded blotches.** Apply slightly diluted walnut stain until reaching the desired tone. Let dry and rub the blotch with an esparto scouring pad. Then, reapply wax to the wood.

▶ **Eliminating stuck-on junk.** Rub it off with ammonia or turpentine. Then apply some window cleaner and clear it up.

Step by step:

1 Apply the solution to the stain or to the whole piece of furniture if you want to clean it completely. Let it dry for thirty minutes.

2 Thoroughly clean the treated areas with a rag soaked in lukewarm water and vinegar.

3 Let the wet areas dry and finely sand the treated parts in order to compact the wood fibers.

Stripping

Stripping is one of the hardest parts of restoration. It requires a whole lot of patience, and depending on what the piece of furniture has been through, we could find ourselves faced with several old layers of paint and varnish. To strip the furniture, we have to scrape off or dissolve the old lacquer, varnish, shellac, etc.

To strip or not to strip?

• **Strip.** When there are too many layers of paint, the paint is cracking, it does not cover the whole piece of furniture, or it is very thick. Also, when you want the wood to be visible, or you want to find all the damage underneath the paint so that you can repair it later.

• **Don't strip.** When you want to repaint the piece of furniture and there is only a thin layer of paint or varnish in good condition.

Additionally, if you want to cover the surface with wallpaper and the layers of paint are not coming off easily enough.

A matter of safety

Chemical strippers and caustic soda, which are used to strip furniture, are toxic and acidic irritants. To avoid potential burns, as well as breathing in any dangerous gases, it is advisable to work in a ventilated area, with a face mask, gloves, and clothes covering the exposed parts of your body. Also pay attention to the leftover bits of paint on the ground: the product may still be activated and will dissolve the soles of your shoes if you're not careful. For this reason, you might want to get rid of the bits of paint by wrapping them in paper or cardboard (never plastic).

Basic equipment

▶ Alcohol
▶ Caustic soda
▶ Paint stripper
▶ Bleaching agent (oxalic acid or hydrogen peroxide)
▶ Card scraper (for stripping sturdy pine and iron)
▶ Sandpaper
▶ Trowel
▶ Old dull knife
▶ Gloves
▶ Face mask
▶ Rags
▶ Steel wool
▶ Brushes: wire, bristle, toothbrush, etc.

Types of stripping

- **Using steel wool (metal fibers)**
  You will usually need a thick one for stripping or scraping and a fine one for polishing. Used for stripping off varnish or thin coats of paint, wax, and other grime, with or without other additives.

- **Using sandpaper**
  (refer to the next section on sanding)

- **Using a horse brush or trowel**
  Before we start thoroughly stripping, we can take off the superficial, chipping layers with this simple tool. Be careful not to scratch the furniture with the sharp edges of the trowel (here we are shown stripping a plastic stool of its outer layer of paint).

- **Using a scraper**
  This is one of the simplest, cheapest, and most eco-friendly methods of stripping, but it requires a good amount of strength and patience to scrape along the grain until you get to the unpainted wood beneath. This method creates no smoke, vapors, or dust, and you don't run the risk of scorching the wood.

- **Turpentine and solvents**

  Used especially for stripping off varnish and wax. We advise protecting yourself with a face mask since this will create a good amount of toxic fumes. You apply it using small cotton rags; let the soaked paint soften for a while, and then strip it off using a fine metal scouring pad before the product has evaporated.

- **Using a chemical stripper**

  Spread it on the wood or metal with the aid of a brush. Let the chemical get to work and then scrape down using a trowel. Because of its high toxicity, we will avoid using chemical strippers as much as we can in this book, although it can be indispensable for reaching corners and thin surfaces that a scraper may not be able to touch.

- **Using a heat gun**

  A quick solution that requires a bit of practice to avoid burning the wood and to remove the paint without spreading it. You should use a face mask to avoid breathing in any fumes or smoke generated by resins or other toxic ingredients in the paint. It is only worth it to acquire this tool if you have identified several other uses for it as well.

- **Ethyl alcohol**

  Ideal for taking off old varnish. It's a cheap, non-toxic solution that will not damage the wood. Apply a generous amount to small areas and let it get to work. Then, rub off the leftover varnish with a cotton rag or a metal scouring pad.

Stripping with caustic soda

Used to strip and clean furniture made from sturdy pine and metal (such as iron fittings) since they can be submerged in a solution of water and lye until all the paint falls off. This method is effective, but it's important to pay special attention to all our safety rules as you are dealing with a potent corrosive.

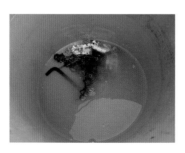

1 Dunk the iron fittings in a solution of water and caustic soda for twenty-four hours.

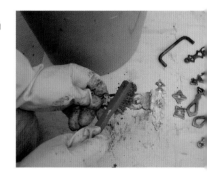

2 The pieces are removed using resistant gloves and they are then scrubbed with a wire brush until all the leftover paint is removed (you may also use a metal scouring pad).

Chemical stripping, step by step

Before starting, it is best to disassemble the piece of furniture to be able to comfortably strip every piece. Your work space should be well ventilated and protected, with the floor covered with cardboard or paper to avoid damaging it and to facilitate cleanup afterwards. Don't forget to cover any exposed body parts, wear thick gloves, and put on protective eye wear.

1 Using an old brush, apply a good layer of your stripping product to the surface you are treating.

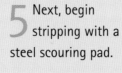

2 Let the product work until the paint begins to soften and wrinkle. (The wait time will vary between five and thirty minutes, depending on the manufacturer and temperature.)

3 Start working on the smoother areas, scraping off the softened paint with a trowel.

4 Continue stripping off the more irregular areas. To do this, you can use an old toothbrush or a soft wire brush to strip off as much soft paint as possible. Use a trowel to clean off any residue that might be left in the brush.

5 Next, begin stripping with a steel scouring pad.

6 If you are unable to strip off all the paint, you can apply a little more of the product.

7 Using a soft wire brush to avoid scratching the wood, remove the last bits that are embedded in the surface. The harder to reach areas can be stripped with the aid of an old dull knife.

8 Finally, clean off the whole thing with a rag soaked in a mixture of lukewarm water and vinegar.

Sanding

Sanding is almost always necessary for preparing the surface. Sanding is done during several steps: when stripping fine layers of varnish, upon finishing stripping, to open up the pores of the wood, to even up surfaces, to remove stains, and more.

This applies not only to wood but to other materials like iron (to remove rust and smooth any roughness) or plastic (so that a finish can bind to it more easily). The sand-

ing step can be done by hand or with the use of an electric tool (mainly sanders or drills with sanding attachments). As a rule of thumb, wood should always be sanded with the grain when possible, beginning with a coarse grit and ending with a very fine grit.

Sand a surface with the sandpaper folded to fit the shape of the piece.

Pressure is applied to the sandpaper using your fingers, not your palm. This allows for better control of the pressure.

On flat surfaces, we recommend using the sanding sponge or the wedge (made of wood or cork) wrapped tightly in a piece of sandpaper.

Sanding of caulking.

Finish with very fine-grit sandpaper.

Even out all the surfaces. (Depending on what you're working on, use coarse, medium, or fine grit.) You can do it by hand or with a tool.

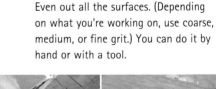

- **Sandpaper and sanding sponge.** There are different levels of quality and grit coarseness. At the store, can find sandpaper with paper, cloth, or latex backings.
  - ‣**Paper backing.** The most affordable and available in all levels of coarseness. Has the downside of being flimsy and tearing easily. Used for small, flat surfaces.
  - ‣**Cloth backing.** Also available in the full range of coarseness. Lasts for several uses, can be soaked and cleaned. More expensive, but more durable.
  - ‣**Latex backing.** A new generation of sanding paper. Expensive but more durable, although it is not available in the full range of coarseness. Similar to the cloth-backed sandpaper, but more flexible and adaptable to irregular surfaces
- **Sanding sponges.** Used often thanks to their ability to adapt to complicated shapes because of its advanced flexibility. They are versatile, easy to use, and can be found in two levels of coarseness (fine and coarse grit).
- **Vibrating electric sander.** Affordable and light. Less powerful than other electric sanders, it is ideal for delicate work. Also useful for flat surfaces, reaching corners, and working edges.
- **Band sander.** Causes a closed band of sandpaper (cloth backing) to spin.
- **Orbital sander.** Sands by rotating a round head.
- **Drill-bit sander.** Used mostly for stripping delicate or damaged wood that needs an extra amount of control to even out the surface.
- **Files.** Tempered steel tools with finely grooved surfaces, very useful for grinding down and smoothing metal and other hard materials. Also useful for working on wood; for example, for smoothing sharp edges.

Caution

Sanding can generate a lot of dust so be sure to work in an open space, or at the very least make sure that everything is covered so things don't get coated with dust. We also suggest using a face mask and protective eye wear, especially when sanding finishes (wax, stains, varnishes, paint, etc.), plastic, or composites that have been compacted using glue or resin that is toxic to the respiratory system.

Sanding by hand or with a tool

Sanding by hand is ideal for any kind of small and/ or curved surface. When sanding by hand, you might want to use a block (usually wooden or made from cork) that you have wrapped in sandpaper. This way, you will be more consistent with your sanding and avoid creating irregularities.

It is always better to sand in a lengthwise direction, along the grain, or in circles. Rarely will you want to sand against the grain, unless you are purposefully trying to damage the wood.

Sanding with tools can considerably lighten your workload, but is harder to control. You'll find tools to be the most useful when working on large flat surfaces. You would usually finish this off with a quick, light sand by hand just to make sure everything is smooth and even.

Fighting Rot

When a piece of furniture has been in one particularly humid spot (indoors or outdoors) it can become the victim of fungus and mold. This bacteria appears on the surface of wood and can end up causing rot in parts of the furniture. The steps you need to take to get rid of rot begin with moving the piece of furniture to a well-ventilated and temperate spot where it won't touch the ground.

Once isolated, it is time to begin getting rid of the rotten wood and parts of the good wood with the help of a chisel. This way, you will be able to guarantee that the new piece will adhere.

A trick to help determine the extent of the damage is to sink the tip of a metal punch into the wood to gauge the thickness or depth of the affected parts (soft and rotten).

Modern treatments

• **Replacing the affected parts.** One proceeds to cut out the rotten parts and replace them with cuts of new wood.

• **Wood hardener.** Consists of injecting a specific solution into the rotten part. It's a type of resin that solidifies inside the holes in the wood, giving it back its strength. When applied using pressure, it will sink into all the holes and gaps deep inside the rotten wood, thereby treating the whole area.

• **Epoxy filler** (a putty or resin made of two parts that activate when mixed). It's used to replace important rotten parts of wood. You scrape off the rot, clean out the leftover residue, and fill the resulting hole, molding the epoxy into shape to replace the damaged piece. Keep in mind that this putty is very resistant once it has dried and can prove difficult to sand. With this in mind, try to apply the putty accurately to avoid having to work it later.

• **Wood filler.** Ideal when the affected area is superficial. To apply, scrape off the softened wood until only hard wood is left. Fill in the resulting space with the wood filler, let it dry, and then sand it.

Bottom of a rotten plywood drawer.

This old file cabinet without feet had been stored in a humid storehouse and suffered damage to its base. Its structure and stability have been seriously affected.

Treating and Protecting against Xylophagous Insects

Woodworm is one of the most common xylophagous pests that can infest your furniture. They are insects that, in their larval stage, feed off of all kinds of wood and attack furniture, leaving holes between 0.5 mm (a fraction of an inch) and 33 mm (about 1 and 3/8 in.). Considered one of the worst enemies of furniture, a single female can lay more than eighty eggs in holes, cracks, and joints.

When the eggs hatch, the pesky larvae create large tunnels through the interior of the wood, eating the softest fibers in the piece of furniture. This "excavation" can last up to three years, after which the xylophagous insects reach maturity and exit the wood, leaving their trademark holes surrounded by sawdust. This is a sign that you must immediately begin applying woodworm killer. First you need to check if the woodworm has left the furniture or if it is still active inside. Look closely at the inside of the woodworm tunnels. If the insect is still active, you will be able to see small bits of very fine sawdust coming out of the holes.

What do I need?
Treatments:

▶ **Chemical treatments** are the most commonly used. You will have to apply the woodworm killing product using a brush to the inside and outside of the piece of furniture. Following this, you will have to let the piece sit for a couple of weeks, completely covered with nylon cloth, and sealed with adhesive tape. The fumes let off by the woodworm-killing product will eliminate any insects left inside the piece of furniture.

▶ You can also get rid of the woodworm by injecting the **pesticide** directly into the holes. You can do this using a syringe or the thin straw that accompanies most spray products. This way, the solution you are using will sink deeper into the wood and soak the innermost fibers. Once the treatment is applied, cover all the wholes with filler that is the same color as the wood.

▶ **Using a syringe**, inject woodworm-killing solution into each hole.

▶ **Using a commercial spray**, inject woodworm-killing solution into each hole.

Caution:

You should carefully read all the instructions that come on the container of the product you are using (dry time, applications, results, etc.) and follow them to the letter. Woodworm-killing products tend to be very toxic and irritating, for which reason it is important to follow the safety and use instructions very closely. While using, do not forget to protect your eyes and skin, and work in a well-ventilated area.

Tools:

▸ **Brushes.** To spread the woodworm killing product, soak your brush and shake it off to avoid annoying drips. Apply to the whole piece of furniture you are repairing, moving along the grain of the wood. Don't forget to apply the product to the joints, edges, and corners.

▸ **Syringes.** If the woodworm infestation is not too serious, you could fight it by injecting the woodworm-killing product straight into the holes. This way, the solution will impregnate even the deepest fibers in the wood and the treatment will be quicker and more effective. Once finished, you'll want to cover the holes with wax or filler.

Prevention:

One of the easiest ways to prevent a woodworm infestation is to cover the piece of furniture in a finish that will provide a barrier and keep the insects out of the wood: wax, varnish, and paint. Another method would be to soak the wood in linseed oil, teak, or waxes that will nourish the wood and keep it from drying out. We also recommend filling any holes with colored wax or filler, not just for aesthetic reasons but to prevent any new eggs from being deposited.

Repairing Parts

If your piece of furniture has been severely affected by rot, woodworm, or moisture, it might have been rendered unusable and be in need of repairs for some of its parts in order to restore function. Depending on the required repairs, we will choose methods suited to the piece of furniture as well as our skill level.

Tools and materials

- **For measuring:**
  Tape measure, ruler, triangle, level, pencil, and glue.

- **For filling:**
  Two-part filler. Used to repair the surface of wood, and once it has dried it may be painted. It is great for strengthening pieces that have been greatly damaged by xylophagous insects or rot.
  Wood filler. Different kinds and colors. Ideal for filling small holes, chips, and cracks.
  Epoxy resin. For recreating parts and fixtures, as well as replacing missing pieces, such as the corner of a wooden tabletop.
  Wax. Solid at room temperature (pure paraffin wax), can be sanded and removed through the application of heat.
  Trowels.

- **For joining:**
  White glue. When in need of a slow dry, this is very useful for controlling with precision the exact position of pieces that have

  been glued. You can also find glues that will dry much more quickly.
  Contact cement. For gluing wood and especially plates and other types of material (carpet, cloth, cork, etc.).
  Hammer, pliers, clippers, tongs, and screwdriver.
  Nails and screws. Always useful for joining and reinforcing different parts of the furniture. For example, it's always advisable to nail down glued pieces in order to strengthen the connection.
  Staple gun. To secure cloth to wood, used especially for upholstery.
  Syringe. Ideal for injecting glue or chemical treatments into cracks and narrow holes.

- **For attaching:**
  C-clamps and bar clamps. For holding pieces in a fixed position to be able to comfortably work them. Also useful for applying pressure to glued pieces.

- **For perforating and chiseling:**
  Drill.

  Gimlet and punch for making small holes.

  Chisel and gouge. For chiseling precise holes into the wood. There are several different sizes and blade types.

  Wood plane. For polishing, smoothing, and decreasing the thickness of wood. It is a thick, sharp metal leaf that comes out of a wood or metal (more precise) wedge that allows you to shave off thin bits of wood. Requires a firm hand and a controlled rhythm to avoid ripping or shaving off too much wood. An electric planer can also be very convenient. Its dual rotating blades can be used to shave off large flat surfaces. It's a powerful tool that should be used with care.

- **For cutting:**
  Ordinary saw. With a wide, strong plate for cutting thick wood (beams, slats, etc.).

  Backsaw. Has a rectangular blade with a reinforced rib along the back for precision cutting. Usually used with a guide to cut frame joints.

  Veneer saw. Small, rectangular, double-edged saw.

  Metal saw. A narrow saw blade attached to a metal arch.

  Coping saw. For delicate pieces and short curves. A very thin blade mounted to a metal arch.

  Jigsaw. Vertical blade saw used for cutting wood, plastic, or metal strips or sheets.

  Guide. For cutting strips at 45 or 90 degree angles. Used with an ordinary or backsaw.

  Glass cutter. The higher the quality of this tool, the easier the cut will be. The best ones have tungsten carbide wheels. Remember that glass must always be cut on a horizontal surface while perfectly flat and immobile.

  Utility knife. Very useful for cutting wood sheets, plastic, etc.

  Scalpel. A precision utility blade for cutting paper and thin sheets.

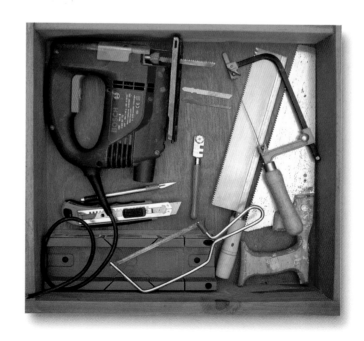

Practical Examples

As well as changing and improving the superficial look of a piece of furniture, we will also learn how to transform it structurally and adapt it for new uses. There are no rules for this; now is the time to let your imagination take over while still keeping in mind a few small functional criteria. You may have a preconceived notion or just experiment until you arrive at a satisfactory conclusion.

You will find yourself facing several possible situations, like getting by with materials you've found with only a vague idea of where you want to go with your transformation. Example: you might recover a bar sign to use as siding for a piece of furniture, giving it a new finish and decorative purpose.

You might look for specific elements to adapt to your project, with a specific end result in mind. When your restoration becomes complicated, you might acquire new parts to achieve the desired result. You might add a board you've already bought if it could work as an important surface, functionally and aesthetically, for a particular piece.

Here we have listed a few useful examples.

Removing and using

The secret to restoring furniture is to have an open mind and learn to find other uses for things. To achieve this, we might add pieces, remove them, replace them, change their purpose, etc.

Example:
A plywood storage box has become severely damaged by moisture and is beyond recovery. Its thick beech supports are still in good shape and could be the basis of a whole new piece. So we will get rid of the rest of the box and focus on the good thick wood.

Reusing and adapting structures

To take advantage of and change the intended use of certain parts of a piece of furniture, we must make changes to adapt it to its new function.

Example:
Here we decided to reinforce the back of this closet in order to turn it into a sofa.

Modifying the layout of a piece of furniture

Sometimes we can change the intended use of a piece of furniture by rearranging some of its parts.

Example:
Here, we have modified the intended purpose of this piece of furniture by rearranging its inside pieces and turning them into shelves.

Adding elements

Another way of transforming furniture is by adding elements that will adapt themselves to their new function.

Example:

A small night stand is turned into a child's desk by adding a cover and a back bar to enclose the surface of the desk.

Adding a wheel

This simple piece can radically change a piece of furniture by giving it mobility.

Example:

Here we have recovered an old chest of drawers and made it fully accessible by installing wheels.

Additionally, this has lifted the furniture up, removing any contact between the wood and the ground.

Adding useful accessories

It might be time to add more function to a piece of furniture.

Example:

Here we've added a metal postcard organizer that has been cut back to fit on the piece of furniture and give function to its sides.

Restoring the upholstery

When restoring furniture it is common to want to redo the seat of a chair or an armchair. One simple and efficient solution is to use upholstery foam and decorative cloth.

Example:

Here we have reshaped a piece of upholstery foam we acquired and we've wrapped it with a decorative cloth cover.

Searching for missing parts

When restoring furniture, you might find that you are missing a part that is important for its form or function. This is when you seek to replace that part by finding a similar part in used furniture stores or parts stores, or even design a new piece based off of what's left of the original.

Example:

Here we have found the base of a table, but it is missing its top. Taking advantage of the recovery of an old drawer case, we will make a whole new tabletop by hand (see the table with metal feet beginning on page 112).

Remaking or replacing an iron fitting

In antique furniture, iron fittings tend to be original, hard to replace pieces. Some of your options are:

–Changing out all of the iron fittings

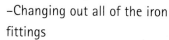

–Mixing the old fittings with some new, different ones

–Reproducing the missing fittings by making a mold. For this, we can use epoxy for metal repairs by making a mold with modeling clay.

Preparing Bases

We know that the finish is the final alteration that will give a piece of furniture its definitive look (color and texture). Finishes serve to protect the furniture as well as make it attractive. But before applying a finish, you must decide on a base for the surface of the furniture to achieve an ideal result, saving both time and materials.

You've already repaired the piece of furniture and now it is time to prepare the wood for a good finish. It's important to invest a lot of effort in this part because it will greatly affect the quality of the end product.

A good base will guarantee the preservation of the whole piece and will limit possible damages, such as dents, stains, and degradation.

What do I need?
- Brushes and rolling pins.
- Rag ball. Useful for applying wood sealer. Consists of a clumped up cloth or cotton balls wrapped in a cotton rag. Then it's filled with sealer and applied to the wood using circular motions.

Sealer or primer

Upon finishing a piece of wood furniture, it is always best to use a sealer. As its name suggests, it creates a seal, closing the pores of the wood and creating a uniform surface that will prevent the finish from soaking into the wood, saving money on paint, varnish, and wax, and better preserves the wood. Before sealing the wood, it's important to sand it well in order to have a smooth and even surface.

Materials

Cellulose sealer. Easily applied (usually with a rag ball), it is transparent and dries very quickly, making it easy to apply several coats one after the other. It is easily sanded down. It can be diluted with solvents to make it easier to apply and covered with all kinds of finish: waxes, varnishes, plastic paint or glazes, stains, etc.

Do not seal the wood . . .

▶ . . . when you want stain the whole piece and not just the top. In this case, the stain must be applied before sealing with sealer and varnish or wax.

▶ . . . when using shellac for a shinier finish. Shellac is a natural extract that can be used as a sealer and varnish at the same time. It is extracted from the lac bug and has been in use since ancient times as a finish for wood. Its use is rather involved, requiring persistence and dedication, although now there are commercial versions that are much easier to use.

▶ . . . when you want to polish the wood. Here, instead of sealing the wood, you are opening up the grain by going over the wood with a wire brush or steel wool.

Water-based sealers. Looks similar to white plastic paint, it is applied with a brush or rolling pin and can be sanded. It dries quickly and seals as well as evening and balancing out the base before being decorated. You should lightly sand the surface before applying. Sealers are the best choice when you want to paint the surface with a dull color.

Gesso. A more delicate primer made from a binder mixed with white lead, used often in the preparation of stucco and fabrics to be painted. It seals and fills the surface with a flexible and resistant finish. As opposed to water-based sealers, gesso can be applied in thick coats to cover, smooth, or create texture.

Rough sealant. The most common sealer when restoring furniture. It is a paste made of fine bits of pumice stone, Vaseline, and alcohol. It's used to give antique furniture a very high quality and shiny finish.

It is applied using a rag ball, exerting pressure and rubbing it into the surface using circular motions.

General sealant. A solvent-based white primer with a great amount of adhesion and coverage. Used in the same manner as an oil-based synthetic glaze.

Primer paint. This paint is very useful as a sealant and grips tightly onto any kind of surface, no matter how hard it is to paint. It is a white, water-based (or oil-based) paint that allows you to paint over melamine, plastics, ceramics, iron, and any other impermeable or slick-surfaced material.

Multipurpose base. This type of paint has several properties—sealant, rust prevention, grip, filler—and is used with all kinds of materials to create an even base that will allow the layers of finish to stick.

Finishing with Paint

Whenever possible, we will try to use water-based paints, whether acrylic or plastic. Binders are watery resins that function as a medium. They dry quickly and are fairly odorless and non-toxic, so they won't be dangerous if you throw away solidified leftovers once the water has evaporated. They used to be less resistant against abrasions than synthetic oil-based paints, but there are currently more flexible and durable paints on the market.

Plastic and vinyl paints

Water-based acrylic paints are normally used to finish roofs and walls. They are easy to use, have good coverage, and feature an ample range of colors (mattes and satins). Plastic paint differs from acrylic in its breathability (plastic is more porous) and its flexibility (vinyl paint breaks and cracks with movement, especially on materials like wood, that expand and contract easily).

Its increased grip, flexibility, and durability both indoors and outdoors means that we can use it without any problems to decorate furniture, as long as we have properly sealed the surface.

Synthetic acrylic paint

This is a water-based synthetic acrylic paint commonly used for decoration. It has the same properties as colored latex, with excellent coverage and a variety of finishes: matte, satin, or glossy. It grips better and is more flexible than plastic paint, making it better for painting furniture. You can buy it already prepared in a multitude of colors, and you can apply it using brushes, sponges, or paint rollers. It is recommended that you protect it with a synthetic or water-based varnish to avoid scratching it.

Fine acrylic paint

Water-based, it has a texture similar to latex. It is thicker and denser than the acrylic paint that is used for decoration and boasts an ample range of shades.

Latex

A water-based resin commonly used to seal porous surfaces, as a medium for binding colors, and as a protective finish. When dry, it becomes transparent and satin, allowing the colors underneath to shine through. There is natural latex (finer and more resistant) and artificial latex, coarser and used more as a base for walls and general construction.

Synthetic or oil-based finishes

This type of paint is commonly used in carpentry and building furniture, or on surfaces subjected to humidity or frequent contact. Synthetic paints are quite resistant and boast

a wide range of colors. Because they are made from oils and resins, it is better to use them in well-ventilated spaces. They dry slowly and need several coats for an ideal finish.

Oil-based paints

Great for adding decorative details, shapes, and gradients.

Dyes

Available in powders or concentrated liquids, they are mixed with

latex, acrylic varnishes, or oil-based varnishes to make paints. In decorative work, they can be used to play with transparency or color saturation thanks to the ability to change the amounts used.

Crackle medium

This is a product that cracks or breaks the layer of paint on top of it, allowing you to see the lower layer. They come in acrylic form for water-based paints and in oil form for oil-based varnishes.

There are also two-part crackling varnishes that can be used to create a crackled varnish finish on top of which you can spread asphalt to highlight the cracks, giving the surface a distinguished antique appearance.

Finishing with Stains

Stains are used to intensify natural colors, dull the appearance of the wood grain, or even out the colors of different parts making up a single piece of furniture. Thanks to stain, cheap wood can be made to look like much more expensive wood and new furniture can be given an antique or rustic look. They are used often in restoration to even out areas with differing colors, such as putty fillings and added parts. They can be used on natural wood to completely change its look, or on the surface of a piece of furniture behind a primer or varnish. Stains also work well with colorful finishes, motifs, or water-based finishes, as long as the wood can be seen through the finish. There are many types of stains, but it is best to opt for an aniline stain that is less toxic and very efficient.

Water-based stains

These can be aniline (water-based) or a general-purpose stain, and come in many colors. They dissolve in water and can be used on natural wood. They will stain the bulk of the wood they are applied to (will sink in a few fractions of an inch deep). Unfortunately, they will open up the grain of the wood when they dry (because of the water content). Once dry, it's a good idea to sand the stained surface.

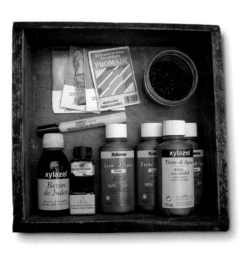

Alcohol-based stains

Better suited to the dense wood (not very porous) of modern furniture rather than the wood of antique furniture we might restore. It is easily absorbed and dries quickly, which may cause the appearance of brush strokes or splotches due to an uneven coat.

India ink

A dark, water-based ink used for decorative purposes in Asian countries. The resulting coat is a very fine matte finish. It has a very intense black color and, when applied using a brush pen, can create very delicate and noticeable motifs. It is important to protect it with an oil-based varnish, as a water-based varnish may blur the outlines of the ink.

Walnut stain

Water-based stain that allows for the reproduction of wood color schemes.

Asphalt

Used for aging new wood, on the inside of drawers or anyplace that will be treated with shellac or varnish.

Stain markers

For small touch-ups on visible finished wood. Perfect for evening the color of filled woodworm holes or other gaps that have been repaired with a filler that is a different color.

Finishing with Decoupage

Decoupage is a finish used in furniture restoration. It is an effective technique for decorating furniture using images, motifs, or textures. It can be done with all types of materials, as long as the pieces are correctly secured and bound. You can use decoupage on every surface of the furniture, as an overall motif, or as small individual decorative elements.

Paper decoupage

Gluing paper can be done with white or cellulose glue (for colored paper). You will usually want to use very thin paper to achieve a more natural look. It's just a matter of adapting your technique to suit the type of paper and testing the sturdiness and porosity of the paper fibers.

What kind of glue should I use?

- **White glue** (for paper, cloth, cardboard, and wood boards). This white and resinous water-based glue becomes transparent and shiny when it dries. It creates a coat that can be protective and impermeable. Should be diluted when applied to paper and cloth.
- **Cellulose glue** (for painted paper). This glue is easy to use and available in flakes that are dissolved in water. Becomes completely transparent and matte when it dries. Once dry, it will easily dissolve in water, meaning it should be protected with varnish if we are going to apply it to the exterior of a piece. It is often used for the inside of trunks, closets, or boxes because it will not give off moisture (perfect for storing paper, cloth, books, etc.).
- **Spray-on glue.** Available with a permanent or removable bond. Does not soak through paper, so it won't cause it to tear or wrinkle easily. Needs to be varnished after use.
- **Contact cement** (for thicker laminates, all kinds of boards, leather, cardboard, carpet, etc.).
- **Epoxy glue.** Recommended for gluing ceramics.

If we use ordinary paper (photocopies and magazine cuttings, for example), we will begin by applying glue to the paper and then placing it on the furniture or object. Next, rub the surface with a rag or brush from the center out towards the edges to get rid of any air bubbles and to smooth any wrinkles. This step must be done delicately, since the wet paper is very fragile.

Another technique consists of gluing the furniture and then sticking the paper to the glued area. This technique can be used with more fragile paper (tissue paper, gold leaf, etc.) to avoid tears when applying glue. Once glued into place, press down with a dry brush to squeeze out any small bubbles, starting at the center and moving outwards.

The last suggested technique consists of gluing both the furniture and the paper and then applying the paper as in the previous techniques. This technique will let you stretch the paper more easily and ensure that everything is completely glued on.

Cloth decoupage (white glue)

An ideal technique for decorating hard-to-strip furniture. You can use this technique for decorating trunks, boxes, or chests of drawers.

Decoupage with gold leaf, silver leaf, and other metals

The type of glue that is used in picture frames or other decorative pieces (molding, motifs, etc.) is specially made so that it will not rust the metal pieces to which it is applied.

Other coatings (contact cement)

We can make an original decoupage using different types of materials like leather, cardboard, metal sheets, sticky plastic, ceramic, and more.

Protective Finishes for Exposed Wood

Varnish

Finishing a piece of furniture with varnish is perfect for protecting it from many external agents, as well as keeping it looking like new. There are several kinds of varnish: alcohol-based or shellac, oil-based or synthetic, and water-based. There are a few guidelines for knowing when and how much varnish to apply.

Nitrocellulose varnish

This a traditional varnish for sealing pores and giving the wood a satin color. It is similar to carpenter's sealer. Once dry, the resulting coat is not too durable, so we advise coating it a few times to avoid scratches in the finish. You can apply this varnish with a rag ball.

Polyurethane varnish

A more durable synthetic varnish, available in matte, shiny, or satin colors. Applied with a brush or rolling pin.

Metal varnish

A type of watery varnish with anti-rusting properties that make it ideal for applying to metal. It has a very shiny finish.

Water-based varnish

A very practical option since it can be diluted with water and it dries quickly and is not much of a pollutant. Available in a wide variety of finishes: satin or shiny, and for indoors or outdoors. There are also some protective water-based varnishes that have been adapted for plastic (anti-ultraviolet) that don't require a primer coat.

Varnish for floors and outdoor use

These are usually very hard and durable varnishes. May be useful for treating surfaces on your furniture that will be well used or exposed.

Colored varnish

There are some types of varnish that will subtly color the wood while maintaining their own transparency.

Shellac

A type of varnish used often when restoring antique furniture. Animal-based shellac (this shellac is made from the secretions of the female lac bug), can be bought in flakes and dissolved in alcohol. Dries into a hard film, shiny and elastic, and provides a high quality finish.

Wax

Restoring wax

A type of solid but oily paste made from animal, vegetable, and/or mineral wax that has been diluted. It protects the wood and gives it a satin look. It works for metal as well, as long as it is reapplied regularly. It can be used with plastic matte paint to give the surface of the piece a silky appearance. It is normally applied with a brush or rag, and once dry it is polished with a brush or wool to shine it. Applying several coats is often recommended. If the surface being finished needs to be water resistant, then you should prime the wood with a special oil-based wood primer before applying the wax.

Calciferous wax

A mixture of white dye, turpentine, and calcium carbonate or white lead. Used for furniture polish, it highlights the grain of the wood or other decorative additions on the surface, as well as protecting the base coat.

Hard wax

Small bricks of colored wax that are used to fill holes after the finish has been applied. They come in a wide range of shades that match with the wood's natural color. When choosing a color, it is important to keep in mind an image of what the final product should look like (which varnish or stain).

Oils

Ideal for protecting and nourishing the wood, they are easy to use but require regular applications since the wood will absorb them as it dries. The most common are teak (smells less but has a lighter color, and is used for hardwoods) and linseed oil.

The oil is applied using a brush or rag in order to soak it as deep into the pores of the wood as possible. Then, it is polished using a fine wool rag, resulting in a durable surface.

Linseed oil

The most commonly used oil, it will add a warm color to the wood as well as protect it from xylophagous insects. It can be mixed with turpentine to thin the texture a bit and so that it sinks into the wood better. Linseed oil can make it harder for varnish or paint to stick, but a wax finish will go on easily. Do not worry about the strong odor of the oil; it will fade away a few days after being applied. Because of the smell, it is recommended that you work in a well-ventilated space.

Proper Maintenance

Tools

Tools are essential for decorating and do-it-your-self projects, so it is very important to keep them in good shape. Purchasing tools can increase the cost of the restoration, but it is a worthwhile investment. If you learn how to properly care for your tools, they will be your best friend when working.

Here are some helpful tips:

- **Chisels and planes.** Must be sharpened and taken care of regularly.

- Separate **tips, nails, and screws** from the rest of your tools and organize them in boxes and cases.

- **Trowels** should be regularly scraped off to clean up bits of filler and paint that may have dried and gotten stuck to them.

- You can store your **tools** by hanging them on a board or in wooden boxes or crates shielded from moisture and dust. It's better to organize them in order to speed up the rest of your work and not have to desperately search for the right tool every time we need something new.

- **Saws** should be stored without bending the blade, and never underneath a pile of heavy tools that could damage them. We suggest wrapping the blade with pieces of cardboard to avoid the blades scratching other tools and potentially dulling the teeth. Hanging them is the best course of action.

- **Rusted tools** should be sanded down and oiled on a regular basis.

solvents, nitrocellulose sealers, polyurethane varnish, etc., and can then spread around and ruin your entire storage space. For this reason, always store them in glass containers (such as mason jars that can be hermetically sealed).

If you move a product to a new container, don't forget to correctly label it with the name, properties, manner of application, and safety measures. Finally, we suggest organizing everything by type of product, so that your toxic materials are all stored in a safe, tightly closed space far away from children.

When storing paint and varnish, the containers should be well sealed with a hammer (by firmly tapping around the edge of the entire lid to seal the can). You can then store the cans upside down to avoid having a solid film of dried product when you open them back up later.

- **Power tools** should be stored in their containers, unexposed to moisture and dust.

Products

At the end of restoration projects, there are often leftover amounts of chemical products that have not been used. Due to the cost and high level of toxicity of most of these products, especially for the environment, they should be stored for future use or disposed of at a site that specifically takes these kinds of toxic products. You should know that most of these products can be stored for an extended amount if time if certain conditions are met: they should be kept away from light and moisture and remain hermetically sealed in containers that have been confirmed to be nonreactive with the product.

Keep in mind that many types of plastic will melt when they come into contact with stripping agents,

Basic Gear

Brushes

There are many kinds and sizes.

Utility brushes

Flat brushes that are usually used for large, flat surfaces. Ideal for textured wood, corners, and edges, a round brush with a tapered end is better. For stenciling and coarser surfaces, a round brush with a flat tip is better. The most practical brushes for decorating furniture are medium-sized, since you will often be working on smaller surfaces with delicate shapes.

Softening brushes

Used to soften and blur the coating of paint by eliminating brush strokes left behind by other brushes. Badger hair brushes are used often thanks to their softness. Horsehair brushes may also give good results at a reduced price, but are perhaps not as well suited for delicate finishes (such as marble imitations).

Dragging brush

Long-haired brushes that are used for leaving drag marks that look like wood grain. Other similar varieties are the speckling brush (made from mane) used to achieve a speckled and mottled look thanks to its long and flexible threads.

Rag balls

Used in the application of wax or sealers (antique varnish). It consists of a wad of cotton wrapped in a folded over cotton rag. Rags that have been used with wax should be kept in a sealed bag. Ones used with sealer should be kept mixed with solvent.

Brush pens

Used for applying India ink. There are many kinds of brush pens that allow for variations in stroking style. They are used for tracing precise designs.

Stamps

Produced using different materials (foam, rubber, etc.) and used for applying shapes or figures over and over again along a surface to produce motifs, textures, or other effects.

Decorator's brushes

Used for painting restored furniture and applying very intricate finishes (hand-drawn motifs, outlines, touch-ups, etc.). Available in many sizes and shapes: flat or round, tapered or flat-tipped, long-haired or short. They tend to be smaller than paintbrushes and made with softer bristles that greatly influence the individual brush's uses.

Brushes with synthetic bristles are not as high quality as ones with natural bristles. The most common brush is the round brush, available in different diameters and lengths. For more precise work, you would use a fine-tipped brush. A flat brush would be useful for applying varnish or spreading lacquer. This wide, flat brush is great for spreading or smoothing paint.

Sponges

Practical and easy to use, they are good for applying thin or diluted paints that are applied in several consecutive layers.

Small rollers

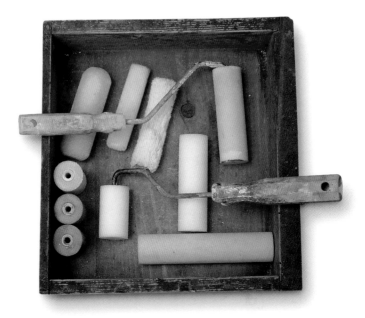

When decorating furniture, we don't tend to use large paint rollers for the obvious reason that they are meant for larger surfaces and not delicate work. We would rather use small rollers made of foam or wool for working on textured surfaces of every shape and size.

You should always work with a paint tray to be able to apply and shake off excess paint before painting the surface you are working with, thereby avoiding drips or an uneven coat caused by too much paint. You can also use a roller to pick up drips or excess paint after applying a layer of very thin product.

Before using a new brush

We advise submerging it under water for a few hours to remove any loose hairs that might get stuck in your paint or varnish. For oil-based painting or varnishing, the brush should be dried well and dipped in turpentine, solvent, or a linseed oil mixture.

Varnish brushes

To keep your brushes soft and flexible, you should hydrate them over the course of twenty-four hours in a linseed oil bath. Oil is a good tool for treating the bristles on your brush.

Leave the bristles hanging in linseed oil for about twenty-four hours. It is important that the bristles not rest on the bottom of the container to avoid deforming them. A good trick is to hang the brush in a plastic bottle cut in half, with a long bar stuck through the hole in the handle of the brush to support it on the edge of the plastic bottle that has been filled with linseed oil (the bristles should be entirely submerged). Afterwards, the brush should be drained onto a towel, removing any loose hairs, and then wrapped in paper that is firmly wrapped around the brush and will help

it keep its shape. When it comes time to use the brush, use a towel (with a little turpentine if you want) to soak up any excess oil and then remove any loose hairs.

While painting

Between layers, make sure you are cleaning your tools thoroughly so that any product left behind does not dry and damage the tool or make it harder to clean later. A few simple habits will guarantee you are keeping your tools in good shape, especially the decorating brushes, rollers, and trowels you are using to apply liquid products that will dry when exposed to the air.

Any paint or decorating brushes that have been used with water-based products should be kept in water in between layers, as long as the in between time does not exceed a few hours. When you are ready to use them again, just drain the brushes of any excess amount of water.

When dealing with oil-based products, you should keep your brushes in a small tin or jar with solvent. They can stay like this for an entire day. If you leave your brushes in solvent for longer, it might cause the bristles to lose their shape and become useless for any future project.

Wool or foam paint rollers can be left suspended in water but cannot be kept in solvents because the roller could fall apart. When you use a roller for applying oil-based products, it will be much harder to clean and will require the use of thinning agents that are damaging to the environment. For this reason, we suggest using disposable foam rollers that are only good for a couple of uses. After using one, you only have to let it dry and then throw it away. This also has the advantage of not contaminating the air and water with paint and thinners. Between layers, you can store the roller in a sealed plastic bag.

After painting

You should always clean your brushes so that they are ready to go when you next need them. When you are done applying your finish, soak your decorating brush with the appropriate thinner (water, turpentine, or a solvent), take it out and then rub off all the leftover paint, varnish, etc. Finally, use a rag to get off the very last bits still stuck to the bristles, careful not to bend them out of shape and always rubbing in the direction they are pointing.

It's always good to finish off with a final rinse with water and soap. There are some oil-based soaps that are highly recommended for washing and preserving decorating brushes. Once clean, dry the brush off well, first with a rag, rubbing along the bristles, and then by hanging it and letting it dry.

Special care

To finish up this list of useful tips, we can't forget to talk about safety, one of the most important things to keep in mind. Before starting any restoring and refinishing project, it is vital to protect our most important tool: our body. Here is a list of essential safety equipment.

- **Latex gloves:** Thin disposable gloves, perfect for applying finishes. They stretch to fit perfectly on your hands, are easy to do precision work with, and will not get in your way. Not good for working with corrosive chemicals.

- **Neoprene gloves:** Resistant against chemical products. They will cover your wrists and forearms.

- **Work clothes:** When we are working with abrasive products and tools that can cause splashes, we should cover our entire body (arms, legs, and feet).

- **Face mask:** You can opt for a filter mask (more efficient) that will protect you from dust as well as toxic fumes, or a simple paper face mask (disposable) which will protect you from dust and chemical splashes. Just make sure that you are working in a well-ventilated space, since the paper mask is not as adept at filtering out toxic fumes.

- **Safety glasses:** Highly useful for protecting your eyes from chemical splashes, dust, and splinters.

- **Shoes:** We suggest working with safety shoes (that have a steel toe), especially when moving and manipulating heavy furniture. Never work with stripping agents or abrasive products if you are wearing open-toed or thin-soled shoes.

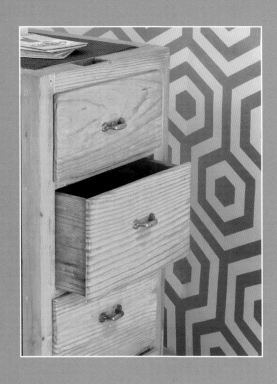

Getting to Work

Plain Colors

Once we have assessed all the damages and determined the changes we'd like to make to our piece of furniture, it is time to get to work. To avoid any unwelcome surprises, we will follow a complete set of important steps. In the first step, we will begin working on the topmost part of our piece of furniture. It is time to take it apart, clean every piece, and get rid of any possible fungi or xylophagous insects.

Multipurpose, Movable File Cabinet

Before starting . . .

This simple file cabinet was found in an old storage room. It was left under an old table and surrounded by unused objects and furniture. We were captivated by the size of its four drawers arranged in a column and the elegance of its antique handles.

The idea

Upon stripping the paint, we find a wide-grained pine wood that gives the cabinet a warm appearance and an interesting beauty. We decide to leave the wood visible and highlight it by coloring the sides of the piece.

The idea is to turn the file cabinet into a mobile piece of furniture by adding wheels (which will also have the added benefit of raising the piece up so it is not in contact with the ground).

Before starting . . .

Assessment

It is made of pine and has been worked on and altered several times: new sides, foundations touched up using different wood, multiple fixes and functional changes.

The underlying structure is fairly deteriorated, and the rotten wood we find in certain areas at the base is more susceptible to moisture damage when it is in direct contact with the ground.

The plywood sides are uneven and have swollen because of moisture. There is some fungus in the bottom of the drawers and it's missing a top.

Technique

We will show how to refinish a piece of furniture while preserving the natural look of the wood, fixing all of its imperfections (holes and blotches) and protecting it with a durable finish. We will also try to reinforce the structure and replace key pieces using other parts we have recovered.

The trick

We will hide the fillers using stains, trying to copy the grain of the wood and avoiding interrupting the patterns.

Materials

For stripping:
- Triangular scraper
- Plastic containers for storing leftover paint bits

For the repairs:
- White glue
- Reinforced pine wood slats for reinforcing and replacing damaged structural pieces.
- Plywood sheets about 3 mm (⅛ in.) thick for replacing the bottoms of the drawers, the back of the cabinet, and one side piece.
- Two boards, one for the top and one for the bottom of the cabinet, where we will be placing the wheels.
- Bar clamps
- Nails
- Electric sander
- Pine colored wood filler

For the transformation:
- Methacrylate plaque recovered from an advertisement sign from a bar/restaurant
- Utility knife and metal ruler
- Drill with a narrow bit and screws with decorative heads
- Recovered postcard holder
- Jigsaw and/or metal saw
- Black staples that are the right size to match the build of the postcard holder

For the finish:
- Wood sealer
- Masking tape
- Strong blue acrylic paint
- Paint brush
- Matte varnish and small foam roller
- Dark brown dye to match the wood
- Thin decorating brush
- Solvent (alcohol-based)

Step by step

1 We will start stripping the structure and the drawers using a triangular shaped scraper well suited to flat surfaces. Scrape in the direction of the grain, dragging and pressing down at the same time onto the painted surface.

Be careful not to tear up the wood fiber: the blade should be kept perpendicular to the surface we are scraping.

2 We take off the sides of the structure. Once we've taken all the nails off, we can finish stripping the joints without nicking the blade of the scraper. We clean the piece of furniture with a soft wire brush to remove all the leftover pits of paint, spider webs, and dust.

3 Now it's time to reinforce and glue the deteriorated fittings. We delicately pry apart the joints without breaking them, tapping on them lightly with a hammer if necessary.

Take care not to break or force apart the other joints. All the matching fittings will have to be re-glued.

4 We clean the fittings of the leftover bits of glue and dust with a metal brush. (If the glue doesn't come off, we can use a chisel.) We ready the fittings by thoroughly covering all the surfaces in glue.

5 We fit everything back together, tapping lightly with a hammer, and wipe off the excess glue with a towel. In order not to put dents in the furniture with our hammer, we can place a piece of wood in between.

6 We secure the glued pieces while they dry with the help of bar clamps and rope, making sure everything is perfectly perpendicular with a triangle. Don't move the piece of furniture for twenty-four hours (the normal time it takes for wood glue to completely dry).

7 Now it is time to work on the structure and top. We will replace the rotten slats with new ones, cut to fit (after measuring the piece of furniture itself) using a guide to make sure we are cutting at a correct angle, and always keeping in mind what we will be adding later and what our final goal is.

8 We glue and nail the new replacement or reinforcement slats, always nailing into the sturdy parts of the piece and being careful not to damage it.

9 We allow everything to dry overnight, secured tightly with our bar clamps.

10 To replace the nonexistent top, we will take measurements and cut out an appropriate piece from our new board using the jigsaw. Don't forget to sand down the edges where we cut. We will fit the top where it needs to go and nail it to the structure (using large nails). We could also secure the top using small 90 degree angle brackets. (See step 11 of "From the Workshop to Your Home" on page 90.)

11 We are going to replace one of the side pieces and the back of the cabinet with thin plywood.

We will take measurements from the piece of furniture and use a utility knife or a jigsaw to cut out two new sheets. The first cut should be done without forcing the utility knife too much, in order to avoid straying on the cut. It should only take three passes before we can simply fold the sheet. This action should never be forced, it's always better to take a few more passes to make sure the cut is clean and without splinters.

Finally, we will nail both sheets to the side and back of the piece of furniture on top of the structure beneath.

12 We secure both sides, nailing them into the structure with small-headed nails every 10 to 20 cm (about every 4 to 8 in.).

13 Now we fill the holes with pine-colored wood filler and glue down all the splintered pieces using wood glue and letting them dry under pressure for a night.

14 Now we have our piece of furniture nicely stripped and with the structure well reinforced. Now we will remove the dark blotches (tannin) using oxalic acid. Once applied, we let the acid dry for half an hour.

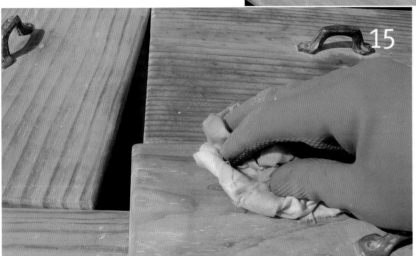

15 We rinse off the cleared up areas with plenty of water and repeat until all the blotches have completely disappeared.

16 We let everything dry and then sand it all down with a fine-grit sanding sponge to smooth the surface of the piece of furniture and ready it for the finish. We also sand, using our electric sander, the whole structure, leaving a smooth feel and an even surface.

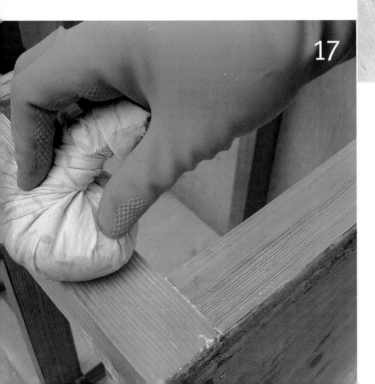

17 Now we've arrived at the finishing phase. We prepare a mixture of sealer and solvent in a small tin. Using a rag ball, we apply the mixture across the entire piece of furniture several times to ensure we have completely sealed it. Let it dry.

18 We isolate the area we are going to paint using masking tape and proceed to paint one of the sides blue until we achieve an even, opaque coat of paint.

19 Using a mixture of alcohol and brown dye, we paint over some of our filler using a fine-tipped decorating brush to make it look like natural wood grain. The idea is to have these spots match the color of the wood fibers. To achieve a good finish, we will use a rag to spread the stain and get a more natural result. You will usually not be able to copy the look of the grain on the first try, but that's fine because you can get rid of your work with alcohol and try again.

20 Finally, we will cover the whole piece of furniture with a layer of matte varnish that we will apply quickly with the help of a small foam paint roller.

21 With a soft scouring pad and vinegar, we polish the iron fittings until they are clean and shiny. We can use a layer of varnish for the metal and avoid all kinds of rusting down the road.

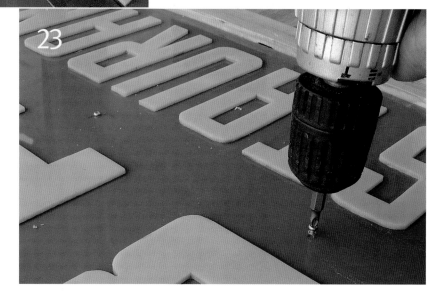

22 Now we will cover the open side of the cabinet with an old methacrylate advertisement sign. We will use the utility knife to mark the first cut on the sign (using a metal ruler), after having taken measurements from the piece of furniture. We will mark the cut several times without moving the ruler. We will lay the piece we want to keep on a flat surface with the part we are removing hanging over the edge. Then we will tap that part until it comes loose. You should never have to force this; if the piece does not come off, then you need to mark the cut some more.

23 Now we fit the sign in place on top of the supports that are in the structure, and we will proceed to drill through the sign (no deeper than 1 mm (³⁄₆₄ in.) into the wood so that the screws can still grip). We secure the sign to the side with several screws.

24 Now we'll work on the second side (with the blue paint). We cut the postcard holder using a metal saw or a jigsaw so that it fits on the side of the cabinet. Make sure the surface you are cutting on top of is stable and does not shake while you are cutting.

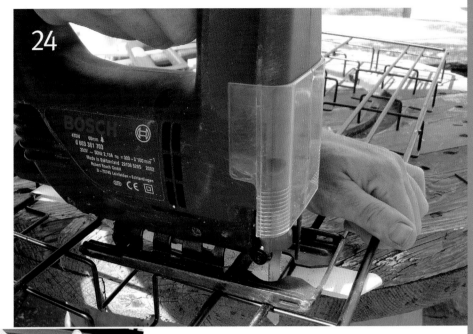

25 Next, we will center the postcard holder and mark its position; then we will secure it in place using electrical staples that fit the size of the postcard holder and staple it into the structure behind the side panel.

26 To finish up the project, we turn the cabinet over and screw in the four wheels.

A Great Small Complement

Before starting . . .

A strange stool with odd, captivating proportions that hint at a creative design hidden behind a banal finish and colors that don't suit its shape.

The idea

We will be attempting to achieve a matte finish that brings to mind a velvety texture. We'll look for a strong color, capable of making this piece a star, fun and worthy of interest. The color of the seat will contrast with the tone of the chair, both in vibrations and contrast (of texture).

Technique

This finish is simple but requires a good deal of work. The secret is in the application of diluted coats that will thin the paint and let it avoid the textures. The varnish will dull this effect a little, but it is necessary to protect the finish which would otherwise gather a lot of dirt.

Assessment

The beech wood is in good shape since it has been protected by a tough, shiny coat of varnish. The cloth on the seat is completely torn up, robbing it of its beauty.

The seat will be easy to replace; you can simply take it off since it is just a piece of composite wood covered in a foam cushion. That, in turn, is covered by a plastic cover stapled on the back of the board.

The trick

Since the finish on the chair is in good shape, we'll opt for a simple sanding with the goal of opening up the pores at the surface and making sure the paint is able to grip. Additionally, if we apply a coat of primer right after, we'll give the whole piece a much more durable finish.

Before starting . . .

Materials

Preparation:
- Fine- and medium-grit sandpaper and sanding sponges
- Rags
- General solvent
- White primer
- Paintbrushes

Finishing:
- Poppy-colored matte plastic paint
- Container for mixing the paint
- Matte varnish

Seat cover:
- Plastic cloth
- Staple gun
- Screwdriver and pliers for removing screws

Step by step

1 We take the seat off the stool and sand the surface of the varnish using a medium grit to scratch it off and open up the pores. This way, our subsequent layers will have a much easier time getting a grip.

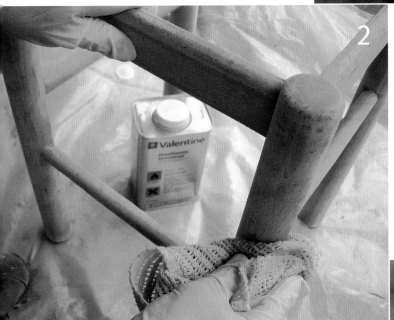

2 We continue sanding the chair with a very fine-grit sanding sponge. We are looking for an even matte finish. We clean the surface with a wet rag to get rid of any leftover dust. You can use a solvent to make sure there is no leftover varnish.

3 Using a brush, we apply a base of primer. It's best not to cover the whole stool with the first coat to avoid drips or a sticky mess.

4 We let the first coat of primer dry and then we sand the whole stool with fine-grit sandpaper. It should feel smooth and even to the touch.

5 Now we apply the second coat of primer, creating an even and opaque base.

6 We let this dry and use a paintbrush to apply a thin coat of red-colored paint (poppy) in a 3:1 solution of paint to water (the proportions will vary depending on the type of paint, its texture, etc.). To make sure everything is of the highest quality, we won't cover the entire stool in one coating. We also advise against loading your brush with too much paint. The thinner the coat of paint is, the faster it will dry.

7 When the paint is dry to the touch, you can apply another diluted coat. We will let the whole thing dry for half a day.

8 We sand using very fine-grit sandpaper, exerting little pressure, until we have a very smooth surface. Afterwards, we'll use a rag to wipe off any leftover dust.

9 We apply another thin layer of paint, less diluted. We'll spread the paint as thin as we can so we don't leave drops or sticky areas that will mess up our end result. If necessary, we can sand again in between layers to make sure the surface is even smoother, making sure to clean up all the dust before applying the next coat. We will let the stool dry overnight.

10 Now we'll apply a couple of coats of matte polyurethane varnish using a brush we've readied specifically for varnishing.

11 We take off the old seat cover without tearing it. We can use a flat head screwdriver to lift the staples and then pry them out with pliers.

12 We'll use the old cover as a guide when we cut the new one. We mark our guidelines on the back of our plastic-covered cloth.

13 As in the original, we'll cut the corners so that they won't bunch up too much when we fold them over for stapling.

14 We center the newly cut cloth on the base of the seat. We start stapling in the middle and move out towards the sides, applying tension to the cloth until we reach the corners.

15 And to finish up, we place the seat back in its place on the stool

A Desk for the Kids

We found this end table at a flea market. We were interested in its modern appearance, with elevated sides, fifties-style coating, and metal legs.

The idea

The uniqueness of this piece comes from its drawer, the true protagonist of the ensemble, held in place by two lateral pieces and supported below by four metal legs. The odd proportions of the base and the size of the drawer made us think of turning it into a small desk. And so, we decided to turn this simple end table into a fun children's desk, adding a third border and a useful chalkboard top that will close down on the desk. We chose yellow because of its warmth and because if looks so good next to the pitch black of the chalkboard, keeping true to the piece's urban design.

Technique

We are going to use a simple painting technique using a roller to achieve strong, opaque colors. Among them, the matte black of the chalkboard finish. Using a few simple DIY methods, we will completely change the function of this table.

Before starting . . .

Assessment

The appearance of the piece suggests that it has been previously worked on. The style of the metal feet does not seem to match the design of the wood. Surely, this is a piece that has been cobbled together from different parts of furniture. Additionally, the gray and white paint does not seem to have gripped the varnish base very well and started cracking and peeling off. The table seems to be very stable thanks to its heavy metal base.

The trick

In order to achieve an even color coat across the flat surfaces, we suggest using a base coat to prepare the table ahead of time and even out the spaces in preparation for the small foam roller we will be using to apply the coats of paint afterwards. In order to achieve a good finish, you should shake excess paint off the roller before each application, spreading out the layers and painting using intersecting strokes. We will also refrain from diluting the paint too much, since the foam brush will absorb too much of it.

Materials

Stripping:
- Flat-bladed scraper

Transforming:
- Plywood board or medium-density fiberboard about 1 cm (about ⁷⁄₁₆ in.) thick and the same size as the tabletop.
- Wooden slat as wide as the table borders and just as thick
- Saw and guide

- White glue
- Bar clamps
- Thin hinges
- Small chain
- Two small eye screws

Preparation:
- Screwdriver
- Medium- and fine-grit sanding sponge
- Masking tape

- Wood sealer
- Paint brush

Finishing:
- Primary yellow colored paint
- Small foam roller
- Paint tray
- Satin varnish
- Matte black chalkboard paint
- Masking tape

Step by step

1 To begin, we will unscrew the knob on the drawer so we can easily strip it down.

2 Now we will strip the whole piece of furniture using a paint scraper. The old coat of varnish that is covering the table will make stripping the paint a lot easier.

3 In order to even the surface and take off any leftover varnish, we will sand the whole thing (including the metal pieces) with medium-grit sandpaper and smooth it out. We'll finish off with a fine-grit sand to leave everything smooth to the touch and even in preparation for the finish.

4 We'll wipe off the dust with a clean rag and outline the areas we want to paint with masking tape to protect the rest of the table.

5 We will begin our transformation before starting the decorations: we'll add a wooden slat to the back of the tabletop create a continuous enclosed top, useful for keeping pens from falling behind the desk. It will also serve as support for the chalkboard when it is closed. We will cut the slat with the aid of a saw and a guide after taking precise measurements directly from the table.

6 We add glue to both of the pieces we'll be joining. We advise using glue from a bottle in order to apply what is called a "glue worm" that will guarantee a perfect stick.

7 We place the piece we are gluing in its final spot.

8 We secure it with bar clamps and leave it to dry for about twenty-four hours. To keep from marking our glued pieces with our bar clamps, we suggest using pieces of wood as intermediaries between the clamp and the wood.

9 With regards to the board we'll be using as the top and the chalkboard for the desk, we advise getting it professionally measured and cut. If you manage to find an appropriate board elsewhere, you will have to precisely measure it and use a handsaw or a jigsaw to cut it to the right shape.

In order to make an exact cut, you should secure the board to a sturdy surface with the help of your bar clamps. Finally, you should sand down the cut edges to eliminate any splinters, and then the rest of the board to even everything out.

10 We apply two coats of white water-based primer to the whole piece, including the top board, the iron legs, and the drawer. A light sanding in between layers is helpful.

11 The base coat should be smooth and even. Let it dry.

12 Using a small foam roller, we'll apply three thin coats of yellow plastic paint over the entire piece. Don't forget the legs and board. Let it dry in between layers.

13 Once it has completely dried, we apply two coats of matte varnish to the piece of furniture and all its parts. Let it dry.

14 Use masking tape to outline the space where we will be creating the chalkboard. It's important to let the varnish dry completely before taping the wood so we avoid damaging the varnish.

15 Using a small foam roller, we paint the designated area with matte black chalkboard paint. We'll apply a couple of coats just to make sure the finish is sturdy. Let it dry.

16 We repaint the handle black and screw in the hinges that will hold the chalkboard to the back panel of the desk. We insert the eye screws that will hold the chain that secures the board.

A Stylish Couch

We found this old base for a wardrobe in a restoration workshop's storage. There it was, just waiting for a new wardrobe that would fit it. It had been there for a long time and they sold it to us at a great price. We were drawn by its large size, carved feet, and the good shape it had been kept in.

Idea

We decided to pick up this wardrobe base to convert into a couch—a low seating area with a baroque touch that will make this piece an elegant addition to a home once we've painted it, finished it, and given it some nice cushions.

Technique

We are going to use a simple painting technique with a brush to achieve a dark but intense and shiny finish.

Assessment

In order to adapt this piece for its new use as a couch, we'll have to reinforce the base surface with some simple wood, adding a series of new slats underneath that will let it hold more weight.

The trick

We were looking to achieve a dark but intense color, and we achieved that with a couple of different paints. We started with a few light coats to bring up the opacity of the base and we finished with a more intense coat of colors that we liked. This classic, cheap technique gives the finish a certain glow.

Before starting . . .

Materials

Stripping:
▸ Paint scraper
▸ Stripper
▸ Fine wire brush
▸ Steel wool
▸ Protective gloves
▸ Fine- and medium-grit sandpaper.

Repairing:
▸ Woodworm killer
▸ Paint brush
▸ Syringe
▸ Wood filler
▸ Trowel

Reinforcing the structure:
▸ Unbrushed wooden slats
▸ Screws
▸ Nails
▸ White glue
▸ Jigsaw
▸ Pliers
▸ Bar clamps

Preparation:
▸ Water-based white primer
▸ Paint brush

Decoration:
▸ Purple-red plastic paint
▸ Dyes for reinforcing the color
▸ Paint brush
▸ Paint tray for mixing colors
▸ Shiny polyurethane varnish
▸ Varnish brush
▸ Carpeting
▸ Ruler and utility knife
▸ Double-sided tape

Cushion:
▸ Foam cut to fit the base and cushions
▸ Pen and ruler
▸ Fabric
▸ Sewing machine
▸ Scissors
▸ Cotton rope for lining the cushions.
▸ Buttons
▸ Strong, thin thread
▸ Large needle
▸ Velcro

Step by step

1 Using our paint scraper, we remove all the varnish from the flat surfaces.

2 We strip the carved pieces by applying a chemical stripper. We let the product work until the varnish has softened.

3 While wearing our protective gloves, we brush the rest of the varnish off with a wire brush. We shouldn't press down too hard to avoid scratching the wood. We'll remove the last bits of stripper and varnish with some fine steel wool. We clean the piece of furniture with a general solvent to get rid of the rest of the stripper.

4 Now we are going to treat the wood against woodworm. Using a brush, we'll apply our woodworm-killing product as well as injecting it with a syringe into every little hole. Let it dry.

5 We fill the woodworm holes and any other chips using neutrally-colored wood filler. Once the filler is dry, we'll sand the whole thing down, using a sanding sponge for the flat parts and a folded piece of sanding paper for the textured parts.

6 The wood board that is covering the base structure is very thin and not designed for bearing too much weight, particularly in the middle. Because of this, we will reinforce the bottom structure using wooden slats so that we can use the base for sitting. We bought unbrushed wooden slats that we can adapt to the shape of our base. We take measurements from the base and cut the slats using a handsaw or a jigsaw.

We also cut some shorter slats with notches that we'll use to reinforce some of the original boards. We will screw those straight into the base. Now we apply a coat of linseed oil to the entire structure underneath our base (this will not be painted).

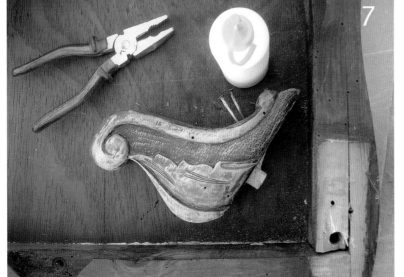

7 Some of the feet are loose. Well take them off by pulling out the nails and tapping the feet until the old glue gives. We'll change out the reinforcing joints that are broken or degraded and replace them with new ones in better shape.

8 We scrub off the old glue using a scouring pad or coarse sandpaper. Clean off the dust. We glue, nail, and secure everything with bar clamps, and clean off the excess glue. We'll let it dry for twenty-four hours.

9 We clean off the whole piece and use masking tape to outline our top board, leaving an un-taped border around the edge. We'll apply two coats of primer paint on all the visible portions of wood, as well as underneath of the outer supporting structure. Let it dry.

10 Now we'll paint the whole piece of furniture with our purple-red plastic paint, diluted with a little bit of water. Let it dry.

11 Now we are going to mix a little of the undiluted purple-red paint with some drops of red and blue dye to adjust the color a bit to suit or needs.

12 We'll apply a couple of coats of this mix, without diluting it, to the entire visible piece. The layers should be thin and spread out to make the surface smooth and even (without drips). Let it dry for a whole night.

13 We'll finish off with two coats of polyurethane varnish, using a brush that we previously readied for the task.

14 Now we'll make some cushions, specially fitted to our base. We could buy the foam already cut to shape, or reuse an old foam mattress we might have lying around, cutting it with a metal saw or a large, well-sharpened utility knife. The cut won't be as clean or professional, but in the end you won't be able to tell the difference.

15 We pick out a sturdy cloth and mark with a fabric pencil where we need to cut out our cushions, keeping in mind the thickness of the foam and leaving enough space on the future corners for the decorative cord we will be attaching. We will also leave a little bit extra to serve as the closing flap.

16 After making sure our measurements are exact, we cut out the pieces as accurately as we can.

17 We sew the cover, attaching our cord on the corners. The top cushions will not have cord on their edges. Their creation will be simpler.

18 Their fastener will be made by sewing Velcro onto a flap so we can take off the cover and wash it whenever we need.

19 To attach the cover to the lower cushion, and to add a decorative touch as well, we will sew on buttons that match the tone of the furniture. To start off, we will place the buttons on the cushion and mark where they'll go.

20 With a large needle and thread, we pierce the cover, sewing one button on the top and another on the bottom so that the cloth doesn't rip off.

21 To make sure the bottom cushion doesn't slip, we will attach some recovered carpeting to it. We take measurements and cut the carpeting with a utility knife. Underneath it, we'll place double-sided tape that will make sure it doesn't move.

22 We can take the tape off as we secure the rug to the base.

Aging Effects

A common theme when restoring furniture is to attempt to imitate an older style. We often seek to make things look antique or well-used, and in this chapter we'll show you the techniques needed to achieve these classic looks and then adapt them to modern colors or designs in order to make them unique and contemporary.

From the Workshop to Your Home

This suggestive piece surely formed part of a wall cabinet in some ancient artisan workshop. It has a notably functional style, with rough wood, an absence of laterals, and an added top. We found it while walking through a neighborhood market and were immediately seduced by its proportions and simplicity.

Idea

Once we've verified the sturdiness of the structure, our idea is to improve the general appearance of the piece. The objective will be to rehydrate the wood, even out the textures, renovate the top, and give it a splash of color and a new, functional complement that will be useful for hanging rags, towels, or tools.

Technique

The surface of the piece of furniture will be cleaned and sanded, and then the wood will be soaked with linseed oil, giving it a warm color as well as protecting the wood.

Before starting . . .

Assessment

At first glance, it looks to be in good shape, even though you can see its degradation and the signs of its many transformations. It's missing the bottom two drawers, but they have been replaced with some wooden boards to turn the space into shelves. The top (a pine board that was screwed in) has also been added to give the piece more function. The surface is a little bit damaged, but the structure is holding firm. When we take off the top, we find loose and broken supports in the structure. The wood is generally pretty dry.

The trick

The wood this piece is made of is fairly delicate and can be scratched extremely easily (with just a fingernail). To toughen it up, we're going to use an old technique that works by applying a lot of pressure to the wood after filling it with oil to harden up the surface. Using a piece of steel wool, we rub the surface until we achieve a desired roughness. This will give the piece of furniture a weathered look, leaving the surface perfectly glossy.

Materials

Cleaning and sanding:
- Paint scraper
- Wire brush
- Sanding sponges
- Electrical sander with replacement pads (medium and fine grit)

For the transformation:
- Round wooden slat for mounting the lateral bars
- Two metal fasteners to hold our round slat
- Top board and plywood

For the finish:
- Linseed oil
- Turpentine
- Red acrylic paint
- Paintbrushes
- Varnish

Step by step

1 We begin by taking off the screwed-in top piece and the drawers so we can take a good look at the underlying structure.

2 We clean everything inside with a wire brush. Then we do the same to the outer pieces using a sanding sponge to get rid of dust, cobwebs, and grease. This is when the damage and imperfections start to appear.

3 Some of the drawer spaces are broken, loose, and cracking. One of them is practically torn out of the front of the cabinet, damaging the look and stability of the structure. Using a chisel, we create a parallelepiped-shaped notch where the break is. To fill the notch, we will cut a pine slat or board to fit the hole. Finally, we'll clean and prepare the rest of the loose slots.

4 We glue and fasten both parts (the notch and the new piece of wood). We also take this time to inject glue into all the other slots. You should be generous with the glue while remembering to always clean off any excess with a wet rag.

5 Once all the slots have been glued, we apply pressure using cords (like a windmill) and bar clamps. To avoid marking the wood, remember to protect our clamped areas with extra wood or cardboard. Clean off all the excess glue.

A botched glue job could be irreversible. Because of this, it's a good idea to check all the angles using a triangle. Now, we'll leave everything to dry for about twenty-four hours.

6 After everything dries, the structure should be nice and sturdy. We take apart our clamping system and fill in any holes, notches, and chips using wood filler. Let it dry.

7 We strip off any paint that's on the iron handles using a trowel or chemical stripper and steel wool.

8 Once the filler is dry, we sand the entire piece of furniture. We start with medium-grit sand, and finish it off with a fine-grit sand, leaving everything even and soft to the touch. We can use an electric sander if we want to make this part easier. At this point, the piece of furniture should start looking good.

9 Now it's the drawers' turn. We'll sand them first on the sides as well as the front.

10 To replace the old top, we've opted for a striped pine board about 2.5 cm (1 in.) thick. We ask the carpenter to cut it to our specifications. Once at home, we sand it well and apply a coat of linseed oil to the bottom. We finish by sanding the top part until it is nice and soft to the touch.

11 We screw four metal angle brackets into the inside of the structure to hold the new top board. We fix the piece in place from below, through the gaps of the drawers.

12 Next, we apply linseed oil to everything, including the new top, the sideboards, the structure, and the drawers. It's a good idea to thin the oil with some turpentine to make sure it fully soaks into the wood (it protects and nourishes it). You should apply it using a brush and let it dry overnight. The next day, you can repeat this process to be sure the wood is fully protected. Once dry, we polish the entire surface with steel wool.

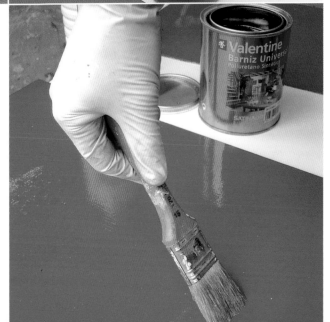

13 Once the linseed oil dries we polish the piece of furniture, moving along the grain with a piece of steel wool to flatten down the grain (without breaking it) and harden the surface.

14 We cut a piece of plywood to replace our inside shelves and seal it with a primer. Then we apply two coats of red plastic or acrylic paint. We protect the finish with some sturdy varnish (a couple of coats). Let it dry.

15 Now we'll place our round wooden slats (perfect for hanging rags or tools) on the sides. In order to do this, we mark the exact placement of our fasteners and lightly drill guide holes using a thin bit to ease the fasteners into place and avoid cracking the wood. We place the fasteners into the wood and firmly screw them down.

16 Then, we slip each end of the round slat, making sure it is nice and tight.

17 Finally, we'll apply a nice anti-rust varnish to the metal handles and nail the two red shelf boards using small, evenly spaced nails.

Magical Transformation

We found this fifties-styled piece of furniture abandoned in the yard of a local artisan. After prolonged exposure to the outdoors, the composite wood boards had been seriously damaged.

Idea

We have our support structure, now all we need are containers. We decided to acquire some metal boxes that slip in between the legs of the base with no problem. This way, we'll create a multipurpose piece of furniture perfect for storing items in the bathroom, or as a magazine rack, a filing cabinet in the office, or even a tool rack that can store gardening products in our greenhouse.

For the finish on the wood, we'll use a crackling technique that will subtly show off the base coat of light blue paint. The base will have an antique structure that will contrast with the modern use of all the elements.

Technique

The crackling effect is achieved by applying a crackle varnish over the light blue base coat of paint and under the surface coat, which will be cream. To finish, we'll protect the entire piece with a coat of glossy polyurethane varnish that will shine the wood and help it resist humidity.

Before starting . . .

Assessment

The major attraction of this piece is the legs and the solid wood base structure. It is also the part that has best weathered the passage of time. The rest of the piece is very worn and will be harder to restore. We'll focus on the legs and get rid of the rest since it will be impossible to bring back to life.

Materials

Dismantling the furniture:
▸ Chisel, saw
▸ Hammer

Stripping:
▸ Steel wool
▸ Solvent and gloves

Treatment:
▸ Woodworm killer

Preparing:
▸ Trowel
▸ Neutral wood filler
▸ Fine- and medium-grit sandpaper
▸ Water-based primer
▸ Small brush

Finish:
▸ Light blue and cream-colored plastic paint
▸ Crackle varnish (acrylic)
▸ Paintbrush, fine-tipped decorating brush
▸ Shiny polyurethane varnish
▸ Varnish brush

Step by step

1 We start taking apart the piece of furniture. Our main goal is to take everything apart to get at the base structure underneath. In order to split apart the top and bottom, we can use a chisel and a hammer to break through the glued wood joints.

2 We preserve the parts we want to keep by using a saw to cut off the protruding wooden pieces that were gripping the top half.

3 Using a hand brush, we smooth down the surface and clean off any leftover glue and lightly sand everything.

4 Due to the difficulty of scraping off paint on the round surfaces, we'll opt for a medium-sized piece of steel wool soaked with solvent. We rub the surface of the wood until all the old varnish is removed.

5 Now we see the woodworm holes. We inject a good amount of woodworm killer into each hole and let everything dry before filling.

6 We fill the woodworm holes with wood filler, let it dry, and sand it all down to even out the surface and remove the rest of the varnish.

7 Now we'll paint the entire piece of furniture with a white, water-based primer. In order to keep a smooth surface, we should apply a couple of coats and sand well in between each one. Let it dry.

8 We apply two coats of light blue paint across the entire structure. To avoid leaving brush marks, dilute the paint with a little water and apply several consecutive coats. Let it dry.

9 We apply a generous coat of crackle varnish across the entire piece of furniture. The thicker the coat, the more evident the crackling will be later. We allow the amount of time specified by the product to pass (between thirty minutes and two hours, according to the brand and type of varnish).

10 We apply the cream-colored paint. We want to use enough paint to cover all the varnish in a single coat. If there are any areas that come out poorly, it's best to let the paint dry so we don't mess up the surface, and then retouch it. We can accelerate and accentuate the crackling process with a hair dryer. Let it dry.

11 We softly sand the surface to even everything out and remove any drips.

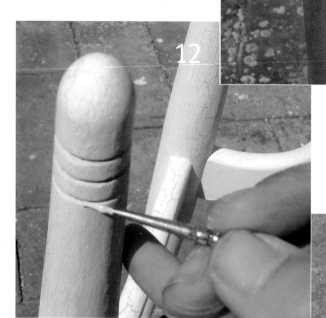

12 Using a fine-tipped decorating brush, we highlight the decorative lines on the legs with blue paint.

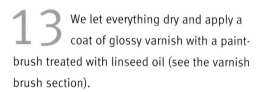

13 We let everything dry and apply a coat of glossy varnish with a paintbrush treated with linseed oil (see the varnish brush section).

14 We fit in the metal boxes, and we're done!

A Charming Desk

We have a simple desk whose basic design contrasts delightfully with the baroque style of the drawer handle.

Idea

Inspired by the chipping on the drawer of this desk when we found it, we decide to follow along with the idea and play around, juxtaposing several coats. We'll use some warm colors for the background (the wood and the leftover reddish paint) and add some more colors that will provide contrast, such as blue-gray covered with an intense turquoise blue.

Technique

Chipping:

This technique gives the piece an antique touch and lets us play with some different coats of color. To keep the realism of the piece, we should apply this to areas of use: edges, corners, holding points, etc.

Decorative strip:

Used to remove paint from specific zones with the purpose of creating a picture (line, motif, shape).

Before starting . . .

Assessment

The piece of furniture has been partially stripped, creating an interesting image on the front of the drawer that makes the blue and green in the upper coats pop. But this effect doesn't appear over the rest of the piece since the legs have been completely stripped, creating an unbalanced look.

Materials

Stripping:
▶ Triangular paint scraper

Fixing:
▶ Wood filler and spatula

Preparing:
▶ Sandpaper and electric sander
▶ Cellulose sealer
▶ Rag ball

Decorating:
▶ Dark gray matte plastic paint
▶ Water-based, marine-blue matte plastic paint
▶ Wax (transparent is best)
▶ Steel wool
▶ Fine-tipped decorating brush
▶ Medium paintbrush
▶ Stripper
▶ Dull knife
▶ Masking tape
▶ Pencil and ruler

Step by step

1 We'll start with the stripping process. We take the drawer out and
strip all the paint we can find with a
metal paint scraper.

2 We perform the first
sanding with our electric
sander to get rid of the rest of
the paint that is still hanging
around and even out the surface.

3 Using a coarse
sanding sponge,
we sand the edges of
the tabletop to even
it out and remove any
splinters left from the
cut.

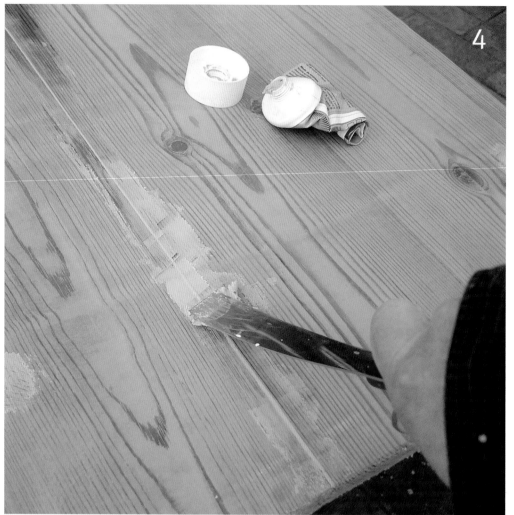

4 Using pine-colored wood filler and a trowel, we fill all the cracks and holes in the wood. We also fill the space that the swelling created in between the slats of the tabletop. We let this dry and sand everything down again with fine-grit sandpaper. We clean off any dust with a damp towel. Let it dry completely.

5 In a well-ventilated work space, we apply several coats of wood sealer using a rag ball or a paintbrush, moving in circular motions across the wood to keep everything even. The sealer is quick drying and will let us apply several layers consecutively. A light sanding should be done before applying the last coat, not forgetting to clean off the dust to keep the surface smooth and soft.

6 With the help of a small decorating brush, we apply wax to all the places we want to leave exposed, especially in areas that will be knocked around the most (edges and corners).

7 Using a medium-sized paintbrush, we apply a light coat of gray paint to every surface and leave it all to dry completely.

8 Using steel wool, we'll rub down all the places we previously applied wax. The paint will start chipping off since the wax kept it from sticking, creating the worn look we wanted.

9 Now we'll carefully clean all of the painted surfaces with a clean towel and we'll reapply wax to the areas that have chipped off. The idea is to widen the areas so the gray undercoat shows up through the chips.

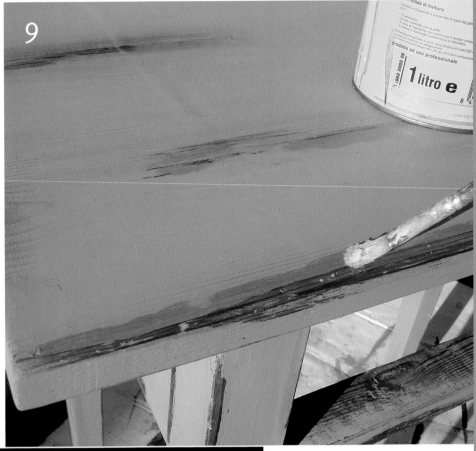

10 Next, we'll apply a nice even coat of blue paint over the entire surface and leave it all to dry.

11 Next, we'll chip off the places we've already waxed with steel wool. Now both of our lower coats are showing through: the reddish wood base and the gray paint.

12 Now it's time for the decorative strip. We use a pencil to lightly trace the outline of the area we are going to strip. Following the outline, we will place masking tape and leave only the area to be stripped uncovered (on the tabletop and the front of the drawer).

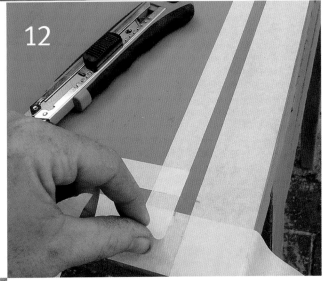

13 Using gloves and safety glasses, we'll use a fine-tipped decorating brush to apply the stripping agent across the line we want to strip and let it act on the layers for ten to twenty minutes.

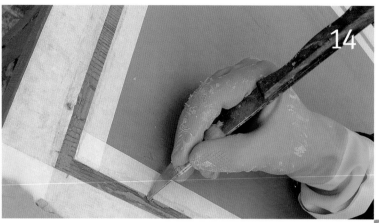

14 When the paint starts to wrinkle, we can start taking it off. First we'll use a trowel or a dull knife, being careful not to lift the masking tape.

15 We finish the stripping process with a fine metal scouring pad to get rid of the rest of the paint. We'll clean off the stripped line with a wet rag to pick up any bits of paint and clean up the stripping agent. Now we carefully remove the masking tape.

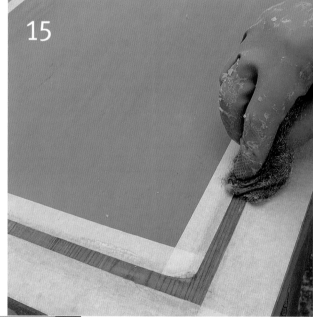

16 To finish up, when the surface is dry, we can apply a generous amount of transparent wax with a rag ball. And finally, when this is nice and dry, we can polish the surface with a clean, dry rag. We can repeat this last process, adding more wax and polishing the area. Two or three coats are necessary for an efficient protective layer.

Table with Metal Feet

These kinds of cast iron feet used to be topped with white marble counters and placed in old bars and cafeterias. They are hard to move and very dense, making them ideal for areas with lots of foot traffic. We found this one stashed away in an old bar's back patio. They probably left it there after breaking the marble top. Its modern design, an art deco inspiration, was our reason for snatching this piece up and restoring it.

Idea

Warm and velvety-looking, the color of the rust (sienna and orange tones) is hard to maintain without the rust doing its job. Normal metal varnishes tend to darken the color of the metal and give it a shiny look that is much too artificial. We thought of several possibilities for replacing the top: tempered glass or a wood tabletop, for example. Finally, when we were walking through a flea market, we ran into some compartmentalized wooden cases, the kind that you would find in old letterpress printing shops. We decided to take them with us to use as a unique dining tabletop, full of small colorful treasures.

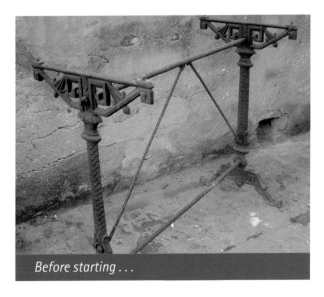

Before starting . . .

Assessment

The feet of this table were in pretty good shape when we found it, but covered in a thick layer of rust. Rust usually can't seriously damage thick, dense metal like this, but it sure can destroy the fine details and decorative shapes. A good anti-rust coating would certainly help to avoid any future, deeper damage. We'll look for a good replacement top.

Technique

The idea is to halt the ongoing rusting of the feet while trying to preserve the warm, matte appearance of the rust itself.

We'll use a metal varnish to create a darker background, but with rust-colored highlights that we'll highlight and accentuate with a grout made from dye that will bring back the natural rust colors. We'll add the dye as we go along to accentuate all the colors of the rust.

The trick

The dye grout will let us reproduce the rust colors by accumulating in the cracks of the metal, creating a realistic effect.

Materials

Removing the excess rust:
- Wire brushes (a soft one and a hard one)
- Bristle brush
- Iron varnish (anti rust)

Protecting:
- Solvent
- Matte varnish
- Paintbrush and decorating brush
- Dye (burnt sienna, primary yellow, iron rust orange and red)

Top:
- Bar clamps
- Brushes and rags
- Woodworm killer (odorless petroleum)
- Electrical sander and sanding paper
- Linseed oil
- Piano hinge

- Wooden slats
- Saw and guide
- Punch
- Screw hooks
- Glass cut to our specifications (tough glass)
- Thread and suction pads

Step by step
Metal base

1 Using a metal brush, we'll rub everything down to get rid of any excess rust, leftover paint, and any other impurities. Using a bristle brush, we'll dust off any leftover dust.

2 We'll halt the effects of the rust by applying a coat of metal varnish. The varnish tends to darken the color of the rust and make the surface glossy. Let it dry.

3   We are going to rebuild the color of the rust, playing with a pale-
tte of dyes: burnt sienna, rust, orange, and yellow with a normal
matte oil-based varnish. Now we'll prepare a solution for our base coat
(the grout): in a tin, we pour a spoonful of burnt sienna color, adding
just a bit of the matte varnish. We mix until we get a homogeneous,
thick paste. We add more varnish (five spoonfuls), mix, and add a general solvent (ten spoonfuls). The resulting solution should be transparent
enough, and you can test this on a piece of paper. On a tray, we have
some bits of dye that match the colors of iron rust.

4   We will paint the iron feet with our base
mixture. It's important not to completely
cover the base. The coat should be light and
the mixture thin enough so that the dye can
accumulate in the corners, just like real rust
would.

5   To tinge the color during our second
thin coat, we can add blotches of dye
directly, using our fine-tipped decorating
brush. We can apply the dye while the base
coat is still fresh, avoiding any obvious
blotches and letting the dye clump together
on the surfaces. We allow it to dry. If there are
bits of dye falling off, we can give it an extra
coat of matte varnish to seal the finish.

6 To begin, we will clean our two chosen cases. We'll remove any dust with a bristle brush and vacuum, and then clean any potential blotches with a rag soaked in solvent. We brush on some woodworm killer to kill off any pests, as well as inject it into each hole.

7 We'll let the killer get to work by putting the cases into a large plastic bag that will keep the fumes in with the wood. We'll let this sit like this for a few days.

8 We fill the woodworm holes and any small imperfections in the wood with a little bit of wood filler, let it dry, and sand down the main structure to leave it smooth and even. We can use sandpaper for each small compartment. Finally, we clean off the dust (best done here with a vacuum cleaner).

9 Now we'll give it a good coat of linseed oil, covering all the wood, especially all the little corners.

10 Now it's time to join both cases and reinforce them horizontally so they can be used as a tabletop. To begin, we'll situate ourselves on top of a flat surface (table). The first joint will be made by screwing a piano hinge to both cases after placing them together, keeping them fixed together with a slat and a bar clamp on a flat surface. The hinge should be screwed in using short screws, and secured into the thickest part of the cases.

11 To provide horizontal reinforcement, we'll add two lateral slats that will go across the length of both cases. These slats will ensure the sturdiness and suitability of our new table. The backing for these cases is pretty flimsy, so it's a good idea to add another pair of supporting slats to the base to provide stability and security. After taking precise measurements, we cut our slats using a saw and a guide.

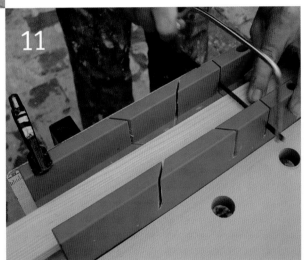

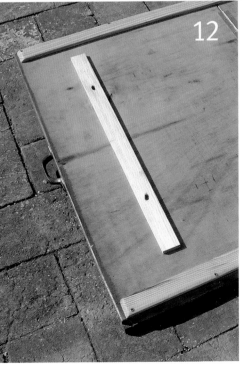

12 We screw in the support slats along the length of the table, always securing them into the thickest parts of the case, using appropriately-sized screws. We'll sand down all the extremities and edges to make them smooth. We will measure, on the top, the exact space where the metal base will support the wood top and place our support slats there and glue them in place. We apply pressure and let this dry for twenty-four hours. Finally, we cover all the slats with linseed oil.

13 To make sure the tabletop stays fixed onto the metal structure, we'll place screw hooks into the support slats, made easier by the use of a gimlet.

14 When we join the two cases together, there are four clearly-marked sections split up by four crossing slats that are raised up higher than the rest of the compartments. This will let us easily fit our precisely-cut glass. As a decorative element, we can place small ornate objects in the compartments (like marbles, colored paper, buttons, etc.).

A small trick: to move the glass around, especially to remove it from where it sits, we'll use suction pads.

A Chest of Drawers from the Fifties

This is a pretty functional piece of furniture thanks to how wide it is, ideal for decorating a hallway. The hand-carved details on the drawers and doors give this piece an elegant simplicity, imitating lines and contours found in nobler pieces. The drawers have an interesting silhouette shaped like flowers and the doors have some flora-inspired carvings as well. The structure in white and the movable dark blue parts give this piece a style that is very common to the fifties.

Idea

We intend to soften the look of this piece of furniture through a radical chromatic transformation. We need a technique that will highlight the carvings by making them stand out against a monochrome background that will cover the whole piece of furniture. This way, the whole piece will be treated using the same technique and color, placing attention on the door and drawers, but highlighting all of its detailed carvings.

Before starting . . .

Assessment

The paint is coming off in several parts of the piece of furniture. The structure is in good shape. If we lift it, we can see bits of sawdust on the bottom, which indicates the presence of woodworm. There is a handle missing from one of the doors.

Technique

The polish will be a paste (opaque) that we'll apply to the piece of furniture and rub down until it dries. This will allow it to sink into all the gaps, cracks, holes, angles, grain, etc. The wax is a perfect product for polishing, since it is just as useful for protecting the wood as it is for decorating it. It is also easy to apply. We are going to make a calciferous wax (white) that we'll apply over a dark blue base coat to lighten it up.

The trick

Choosing our base is key. If the wax is light colored, we'll move towards darker colors that will show up against the wax and highlight all the textures that we like. But there are a thousand different combinations and contrasting colors. And remember that the more porous the surface is, the more the base color will be affected by the wax color.

Materials

Taking apart the iron fittings:
- Dull chisel
- Trowel
- Pliers

Stripping:
- Paint scraper
- Dull knife with a blunt tip
- Stripper
- Old brush
- Steel wool
- Caustic soda

- Fine wire brush
- Chemical-resisting gloves
- Vinegar, lukewarm water, container

Treatment:
- Woodworm killer

Fixing:
- Wood filler
- Trowel

Preparing:
- Fine- and medium-grit sandpaper

Finish:
- Gray-blue matte plastic paint
- Paintbrush and decorating brush
- Rag ball and rags
- Calciferous wax (white lead, wax, white dye, turpentine and a glass jar with lid)
- White anti rust paint

Step by step

1   We'll begin by taking apart the piece of furniture, taking off the doors and drawers. We'll also remove all the iron fittings.

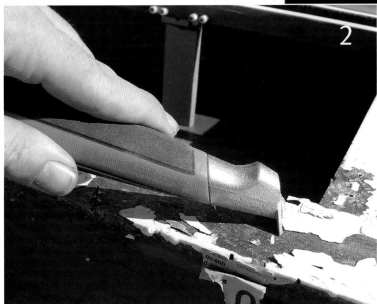

2   Now we'll move on to the stripping phase. The old coat of paint is very thin and ends up being very easy to take off with a scraper.

3 On the carved areas, we can use a little bit of chemical stripper to get rid of the more stubborn bits of paint. We just apply the stripper using a small brush and let it work for about ten minutes (depending on the brand).

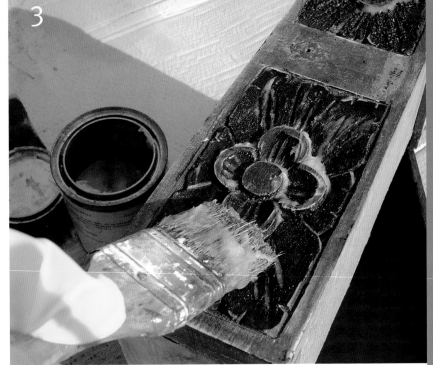

3

4 With a small brush or a plant-based scouring pad, we rub off the softened paint. We can remove anything that's left with steel wool.

4

5 After stripping, we inject woodworm killer directly into any holes and we brush more woodworm killer onto the hidden parts of the piece that we won't be decorating.

5

6 Once it's good and dry, we fill all the woodworm holes and chips with wood filler, trying to replicate the look of any of the carved areas that might have been damaged.

7 We let everything dry and finish our repairs by sanding the whole chest of drawers, especially the carvings where we've used wood filler. We let the wood filler dry and sand everything. We'll fold our sandpaper to reach into the carved wood. We could also roll a small piece up into a tube to reach into the texture and sand without ripping out any of our filler.

8 We glue the front of the broken drawer, squeezing in glue and applying pressure for at least one night while it dries.

9 In order to open up the pores of the wood and accentuate the look with our calciferous wax, we'll rub all the wood down with a medium-sized piece of steel wool soaked in a mixture of lukewarm water and vinegar.

10 Now we'll begin decorating. We dilute the dark blue paint in a 2:1 paint to cold water mixture and mix well. We start painting the piece of furniture using short brush strokes and going over each area only one time to allow the wood to show through.

11 We let this dry and get our calciferous wax ready. In order to do that, we dissolve the white dye in a little bit of turpentine until it's all incorporated. We mix the resulting paste with wax, adding our calcium carbonate or white lead little by little until achieving a creamy consistency.

12 When the coat of blue paint has dried, we'll use a brush (or rag ball) soaked in our calciferous wax to apply the mixture over every surface, paying special attention to the textured and carved areas.

13 Next, we'll rub the waxed surface with a clean towel to take off any excess wax, leaving behind a smooth polish. We'll let the textured areas keep a little extra wax. We try to be consistent with the amount of product we apply and the motions we use, to achieve a homogeneous result. We repeat the process to be sure the wood is fully protected.

14 We submerge the iron fittings in caustic soda (diluted with water) for twenty-four hours. During this time, the paint will fall apart, making it much easier to remove with a wire brush. Remember to cover your hands well and avoid splashing yourself.

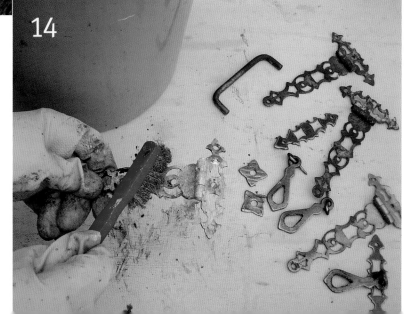

15 We paint the handles and hinges with some white anti-rust paint. You should apply several layers. We let this dry, trying to minimize contact with other surfaces.

16 We put the handles and the hinges back on, using the same nails.

17 As a last touch, we paint the nails and touch up the hinges with a small decorating brush.

Motifs

Motifs have always been the main protagonist of decorations. There are a multitude of techniques and styles belonging to different eras or situations. In this chapter, we'll show some interesting examples you can try at home; geometric shapes, linear brush strokes, descriptive images both stylized and abstract, and unique little touches that will give your restored furniture character and personality.

The New Trunk of Memories

We bought this trunk from a seller and restorer of for old furniture. It's a simple piece with a flat top, ideal for holding objects. It would also be very practical thanks to its storage capacity.

Idea

We will completely change the look of this antique trunk by coloring it fuchsia, a dark and brilliant tone, which we will contrast against the natural clear color of the structure. Over the base coat, we'll paint some continuous silver plant motifs that will stretch across the entire trunk, appearing as though it were also growing beneath the darker wooden slats.

Technique

The hard part about drawing the plant motifs is spreading them out evenly along the entire surface of the trunk, keeping in mind that patterns should be semi random and hand drawn. Because of this, we advise making a sketch ahead of time that will show the proportions and frequency of your motif. Then, we'll trace the idea onto the trunk, using a fabric pencil that will come off easily. By drawing everything by hand, our motif will have a warm sort of irregularity. We will also show how to wrap the inside in decorative paper.

Assessment

Aside from the twisted or broken iron fittings, the trunk seems to be in pretty good shape. But after looking closer, we can see that under the interior cover, the wood is very rotten and seriously infested with woodworm. The interior paper also seems rotten, full of blotches, holes, and scratches. The outside surface of the trunk has been treated with oil-based paint that gave the whole thing a much-too-rigid look. Some parts of the cover are damaged or coming off because of the state of the wood.

The trick

Choosing a color is a very important part of this transformation. We've opted for showing off our trunk by drawing a nice motif that will wrap around the entire piece, making it much more pleasing to the eye. The dark color of the base will absorb light while the motifs will reflect it, causing them to really catch the eye. The random flowers will give it the final touch.

Before starting . . .

Materials

Repairing and reinforcing the structure:
- Screwdriver and pair of pliers for removing the iron fittings and unnecessary nails.
- Woodworm killer
- Paintbrush and syringe
- Plywood strips
- Utility knife or jigsaw
- Ruler and pencil
- Linseed oil
- White glue in a bottle
- Small nails
- Bar clamps and pieces of wood to protect the backing

Changing the iron fittings:
- New iron fittings
- Round-headed bolt screws

- Washers (very important for preventing the bolts from sinking into the wood)
- Drill with a bit the same width as the bolt screws
- Flat wrench for tightening the nuts onto the bolts

Interior paper:
- Red-colored decorative paper
- Cellulose glue for colored paper

Preparation:
- Water-based primer
- A medium-sized paintbrush and a small paintbrush

Decorative finish:
- Acrylic fuchsia paint
- Liquid red and blue dyes
- Masking tape
- White pencil
- Silver oil-based paint
- Thin decorating brush
- Matte oil-based polyurethane varnish
- Foam roller

Step by step

1 To begin, we'll take off all the broken iron fittings as well as any unnecessary nails. We try to do it carefully to avoid damaging the wood.

2 Since the base structure of the trunk has been pretty damaged by woodworm infestation and rot, we take off the most rotten crosswise slats and soak everything with a woodworm killer.

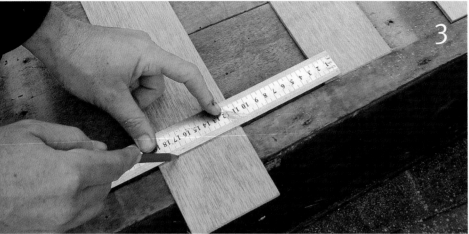

3 Using a jigsaw or a utility knife, we cut several strips of plywood that will help reinforce the damaged base structure without having to replace it all. They should be the right size to be in complete contact with all the rotten wood.

4 Now we'll brush all the visible wood and the strips of plywood with linseed oil. We'll let it dry for twenty-four hours.

5 We start gluing the crosswise strips and the base to guarantee everything is solid.

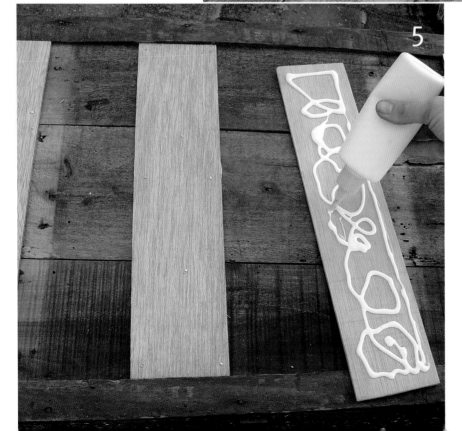

6 As we go along gluing the strips of wood, we can nail them as well, with nails short enough so that they won't poke through. This way, the glue will be much stronger.

7 We want to lift the trunk up a little so it's not directly touching the ground, so we glue some more strips of plywood along the outer edge of the bottom. We will nail these in just like we did before and let it dry for twenty-four hours.

8 Now it's time for the finish. After cleaning the outer painted layer and wiping off all the dust with a damp rag, we can start applying our base coat of primer. We will need several coats so that the surface is opaque, even, and without drips or buildups. Let it dry.

9 Using a paintbrush, we apply two coats of fuchsia acrylic paint diluted in water (3:1). Let it dry for a few hours.

10 Apply some less diluted coats, with a few drops of red dye added to reinforce the color. We are trying to aim for a solid, even color, but not totally opaque. We'll keep a little of the mixture for later touch-ups. We'll let it dry for a night.

11 Using masking tape, we cover the structural wood slats so we can paint them later with a different color.

12 In some of the mix we saved from before, we'll add some drops of red and blue to darken the color. Using a smaller paintbrush, we paint all the slats, careful not to leave any unpainted edges or corners. We'll apply a second coat if necessary. We allow everything to dry and delicately take off the masking tape to avoid tearing the fuchsia paint. If we do tear the paint, we can touch it up with some of the mixture we saved before.

13 Now we move on the picturesque motifs. Using an easily erased white pencil, we outline our plant motif across the entire trunk. The motif should be spread out fairly evenly. We start by drawing our stalks since they will be the base of our motif, and then we'll add the leaves, trying to keep them about the same size.

14 Using our silver paint and a fine-tipped decorating brush, we start painting over the stalks of our motif.

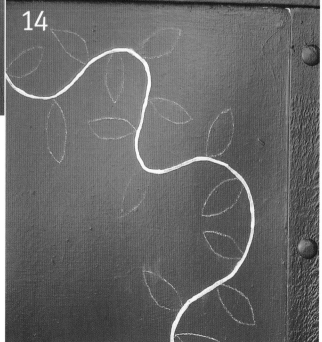

15 Now we'll contour and fill in the leaves.

16 We'll trace out some flowers in some of the open spaces. We mix up some paint, somewhere between fuchsia and pink (using our fuchsia paint and some white), and paint the petals of a rose.

17 In the middle of the flower, following the structure of the petals, we'll add some brushes of fuchsia and spread it outward, leaving the center of the flower a little darker.

18 To finish, we'll add a shine to each petal with a bit of white paint.

19 We let everything dry and then clean off any leftover pencil marks with a damp towel.

20 We apply a couple of coats of matte oil-based varnish across the outside of the trunk using our foam roller.

21 Now we'll move on to replacing the iron fittings. We'll choose some silver fittings that go well with the trunk. When the varnish is good and dry, we'll mark the holes where our handles and hinges will go. We drill some guide holes with an appropriately sized bit.

22 We attach our fittings using the bolt screws and screw down the nuts on the inside of the trunk.

23 Now we'll start adding the interior paper cover. We are trying to keep some of the old paper, so we'll be using the new paper to apply patches along the torn up parts and leave the rest of the old paper visible. To begin, we'll coat the old paper using cellulose glue for colored paper.

24 For the new paper, we chose two styles, a matte one and a lighter one that matched the trunk a bit. We cut out our patches in squares and place them inside in an alternating pattern.

25 Using a checkerboard pattern, we place our new pieces of paper inside. We apply glue to the piece of paper and then place the paper inside. We glue them one by one, leaving the old paper that is in good shape where it is.

An Art Deco Touch

A robust structure with straight lines and mixed with curves gives this piece an art deco feel typical of the twenties. Somewhere between a stool and a chair, this is a multipurpose piece of furniture that could just as easily be a leg rest, stool, chair, or armchair. Additionally, it is very stable and easy to move.

Idea

To cover up the woodworm damage, we'll apply a good filler. Our first idea for covering the filler was to color the piece with some black lacquer to achieve an Oriental look. But upon seeing the beautiful golden-colored wood of the piece, we decided to use black only for the motifs, standing out against the rest of the wood. We decided to create some intricate plant motifs, using repeating symmetry but not a repeating shape.

Technique

Using India ink is a great method for drawing intricate pictures. It is a strong but natural ink that is easy to use and clean (with water). When it dries, it leaves a matte, absorbent surface that meshes perfectly with the texture and color of the wood. Since it dissolves in water, we'll want to apply some coats of oil-based varnish to protect it.

The trick

The basic thing about working with India ink is to seal the wood really well after a light sand to avoid the ink spreading through the wood fibers.

Assessment

Pretty solidly built, the surface of the wood is in fairly bad shape, with paint drips and blotches, meaning we have to strip it well. When we strip the paint off, we see that it has already been restored several times for wood-worm infestations and small defects in the wood. Many of the holes have been filled with white filler or red wax. The seat is in good shape, but it's covered in synthetic paint stains that are hard to get off. We'll opt for covering it with something different.

Before starting . . .

Materials

Stripping:
- Paint scraper

Repairing:
- Wood filler
- Thin trowel
- Sanding sponge and sandpaper
- Electric sander

Cleaning:
- Oxalic acid in flake form

- Lukewarm water
- Rag
- Gloves and safety glasses

Preparation:
- Wood sealer
- Rag ball

Finish:
- India ink
- Brush pen

- Fine-tipped artist's decorating brush
- Oil-based matte polyurethane varnish
- Screwdriver for prying out the old staples and nails in the seat
- Upholstery fabric
- Staple gun
- Scissors

Step by step

1 The old paint is so thick that we've opted for removing it by hand with a paint scraper. Upon stripping, we start finding old woodworm damage. We sand it down to take off any bits of paint and smooth the wood.

2 We're going to lighten the artificial mahogany color of the wood with an oxalic acid solution. In a container (not made of metal), we mix a bit of lukewarm water with oxalic acid crystals, adding the acid bit by bit until the solution is saturated, meaning that the crystals can no longer dissolve. We'll let this sit for about ten minutes.

Then, we apply the solution using a synthetic-hair paintbrush and let it sit for thirty minutes. The oxalic acid is very toxic and corrosive and should be used with extreme caution, in a well-ventilated area, and with protective gloves and glasses.

3 After drying, we'll clean the cleared up areas with a clean rag and plenty of water. You could also use vinegar. It's very important to get rid of any leftover acid since it could damage the finish. Let it dry. Repeat the process if necessary, until all the blotches have disappeared. Let everything dry and apply woodworm killer to the entire piece of furniture (using brushes and syringes).

4 Now we fill the holes, as well as any other chips we find after stripping, with a wood filler that matches the wood. We wipe off any excess.

5 Once the filler is dry, we sand it down with sandpaper or our electric sander, evening out the entire surface and leaving it smooth and devoid of any splinters.

6 Using a rag ball, we apply three coats of primer to keep the ink from spreading through the wood fibers. We make circular motions with the rag across the surface of the wood, leaving no drips or buildups.

7 Using an illustration we found in a botanical encyclopedia, we try to copy the pattern we like onto a piece of paper. We try to keep the sizes all the same so that the drawing can fit on the parts of wood we'll be decorating. We simplify the source image and keep only what we really want.

8 Now, we'll copy the image onto the front of the legs. We trace with a pencil first, outlining the parts we'll color in with black (the outside of the image, as the inside will remain clear). Afterwards, we can add detail to the shapes inside the outline. We suggest tracing the outline directly onto the wood using a pencil, incorporating any defects in the wood into the image. We aren't trying to exactly copy the picture, just adapt it so it fits the piece of furniture better. It's important to maintain balance between the images and the furniture, centering the drawing and paying attention to its height and proportions.

9 Using a brush pen, we draw the outline by hand, trying not to shake and keeping any sleeves away from the areas we've already painted. The ink will dry in minutes.

10 We'll continue drawing with our brush pen dipped in India ink, carefully filling in the narrow edges and corners of the drawing. The brush pen, in situations like this, proves to be more easily controlled and just as precise as a decorating brush.

11 Using a fine-tipped brush, we fill in the rest of the black background, allowing the image to shine with the color of the wood beneath.

12 Using the brush pen, we add small details that will bring our drawing to life (the lines inside the leaves and flowers, etc.).

13 We repeat the process on the front of the other legs, using different drawings of plants, stretching them out a bit to fit on the thin wood. On the crossbars, we need to adapt the image to the horizontal wood and find symmetry by marking the center of the stool. We've chosen a climbing plant to place on this area. The flowers will mark the middle.

14 The lower crossbar is too narrow to draw a very detailed image. Our solution is to use a smaller motif, regularly repeated across the wood to bring life to the black color.

15 On the sides, we add a small black detail: a flower.

16 The filled holes that have not been covered by black ink should be camouflaged and stained with the color of the wood. We'll apply dye to these areas, the same color as the wood, and darken as needed to match the tone. We use a fine-tipped brush to apply the dye and clean up with a rag. We repeat the process until we've completely covered the patches.

17 To finish, we apply a matte coat of varnish to protect the whole surface. We recommend at least two coats.

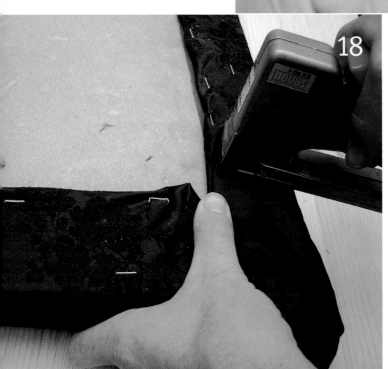

18 If the old seat is in good condition, we can keep it and just replace the fabric. We cut out a piece of tough cloth, taking our measurements directly from the piece of furniture, and leaving a little extra to make sure our staples can get a good grip. We cut out the corners, making sure they won't bunch up too much when we staple them. Starting at the middle, we pull the cloth taught and start stapling. We keep this up, going around the seat and stapling at even distances. We finish with the corners, with as thin a fold as we can manage. Finally, we place the seat back in its place.

Seventies-Style Stool

The iconic Tam Tam stool (Henri Massonnet, 1968). This is a light piece of furniture made from two identical pieces of plastic secured to each other in an hourglass shape. Its design has not gone out of style. It is still a good-looking, functional, and, above all, sturdy piece. This is why it has found its way into our hands. It just needs a little love and creativity to be like new again, or even better.

Idea

We will apply a decorative finish to hide the small defects that we've found on this overall brilliant stool. Its bi-concave shape has inspired a spiral-shaped silhouette. For this reason, we'll apply a finish using a brush strokes that will bring to mind expressionist or impressionist paintings, create movement, and increase the dynamism of this piece. We will be able to make use of a wide range of brushes (short, fine, wide, etc.) for this project, a skill which we could carry over to painting walls if we wished.

Technique

We'll apply a series of lines via juxtaposed brush strokes, using a wide range of different tones of a single color: blue. After roughing up the plastic surface just a little bit, we'll add on an essential coat of primer to make sure our finish sticks and does not chip away.

Before starting . . .

Assessment

The plastic of the stool has weathered the passage of time with no problems. But someone has given it an extra coat of paint that is peeling in certain places. Under the paint we can see some scratched up areas and some other burnt places, probably done by some chemical agent.

Materials

Stripping:
▸ Trowel

Preparation:
▸ Fine- and medium-grit sandpaper
▸ Primer paint
▸ Paint brush
▸ Clean rag

Finish:
▸ Pencil and masking tape
▸ Thin decorating brush
▸ Different shades of matte blue plastic paint
▸ Oil-based matte varnish
▸ Varnish brush

The trick

In order to get a good finish, our method will involve using masking tape to serve as a guide for marking lines on the curves of this bi-concave stool.

Step by step

1 To start, we need to remove all the chipping paint using a trowel (being careful not to scratch the plastic).

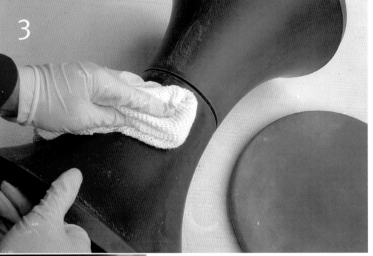

2 We sand down the entire surface with fine- and medium-grit sandpaper until everything matches. Everything should be uniform when we're done. This process will also roughen up the plastic and ensure that our coats of paint are able to fully grip the stool.

3 We wipe off the resulting dust with a clean rag soaked in liquid soap. You could also use vinegar to degrease the stool.

4 We take off the top of the stool and apply a coat of primer to all the exterior surfaces. We spread the coat out to avoid drips and buildups. The first coat should never be opaque.

ValTODO

5 We sand this first coat using fine-grit sandpaper.

6 Then, we apply more coats of primer until we have an even and totally opaque background. Let it dry for twenty-four hours.

7 Using our masking tape, we tape lines that will be our guide for painting on the finish. In order to work well with the curvature of the stool, we'll divide the top base into four parts and, starting from each split, run tape down to the corresponding mark on the bottom base. Don't apply the tape too close together to avoid ripping off primer when we remove it. Using a pencil, we mark the outline of the tape and carefully take it off.

8 We'll start painting with a fine-ti-pped brush, following our pen-cil-marked lines carefully and by hand. The thickness of the ribbons will have to match the diameter of the stool, thin in the middle (which is very narrow) and wider at the ends. We'll start painting the top of the stool with one color, applying several coats until it's solid.

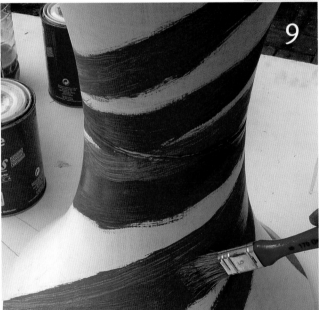

9 Using another shade of blue, we follow our first rib-bon. We're not trying to cover the entire background in one go, we want to have nice thin coats that will let the colors of the different shades bleed into each other.

10 We repeat the process, following our new ribbons with new shades of blue until we've painted everything.

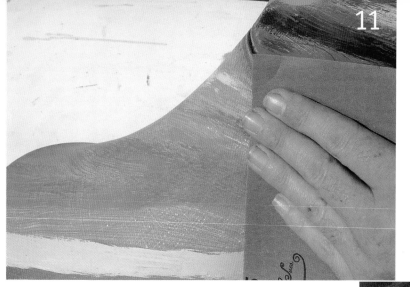

11   When it's completely dry, we'll sand the whole thing down with very fine-grit sandpaper and clean off all the dust with a damp towel.

12   We apply a second coat of paint, using the same colors on the same lines as before. Now we'll use a smaller decorating brush.

13   We go over the colors until they are nice and solid. Using a small brush dipped in water, we will lightly start blurring the edges in between the different shades.

14   We let everything dry for the night and apply two coats of matte varnish using a varnish brush. Finally, we let the stool dry in a dry, clean area.

A Small Table with Motifs

We bought this small but elegant and unrestored table at an antique shop. We were persuaded by its simple design and the good shape it was in.

Idea

Once we began stripping the old varnish off, we found a warm-colored wood that we wanted to keep visible. The composite wood top is harder to strip, so we'll use this area to create an abstract composition using green and purple stamps. The end result will look like a painting on four feet and will be so simple to achieve that it would be fun to have the kids help out.

Technique

In the middle of the tabletop, we'll paint an abstract composition of stamps, playing with green and purple colors. These stamps can be made with all kinds of materials and objects that will leave interesting marks on the wood. In order to do this, we'll apply a base coat of primer.

Before starting . . .

Assessment

Overall, this small table is in pretty great shape, aside from some chips in the varnish. The base is made from dense wood and the tabletop is composite wood secured to a pine frame. During the stripping process, we'll see some black tannin blotches in the wood grain. This is natural and we'll be able to get rid of it by using oxalic acid on the affected surfaces.

The trick

The only hard part in this process will be the tabletop: choosing shapes and colors. Above all, we don't want to go overboard with the amount. Choosing a theme will help us when it comes time to come up with shapes that we want to stamp. We decided to go with a combination of flowers and stars. As far as color, a monochromatic range proves to be very efficient, especially when contrasting against a complementary color (here the purple of the background will complement the green). But before we start, we need to protect the wood with several coats of wood sealer.

Materials

Stripping:
- Paint scraper (flat or triangular)
- Electric sander
- Fine- and medium-grit sandpaper

Repairing:
- White glue
- Rope for applying pressure to the glue

For removing the tannin blotches:
- Oxalic acid
- Synthetic hair paintbrush

Readying the background:
- Masking tape
- Water-based primer
- Paint brush
- Wood sealer
- Rag ball

For the finish:
- Plastic paint in several shades of green
- Burgundy plastic paint
- Objects made from foam or cloth (bubble wrap, foam brush, foam roller, cut up paint roller foam, textured plastic, and a plastic vase)
- Matte polyurethane varnish mate
- Foam roller and paint tray

Step by step

1   We start by stripping the varnish off the piece of furniture using a paint scraper, avoiding the composite tabletop.

2   We keep working on the wood with an electric sander. We sand off the rest of the varnish and smooth down the entire wood surface.

3 We will also sand the painted tabletop to open up the pore of the wood and even it out.

4 Some black blotches appear after sanding off the wood. These blotches are normal (tannin) in wood and can be removed with oxalic acid.

5 We apply the oxalic acid to the affected wood. We allow it to sit for about twenty-five minutes and wash it off with plenty of water. Let it dry and then sand with a soft sanding pad. We repeat the process until all the blotches have disappeared.

6 Next, we apply transparent wood sealer to all the visible parts of the piece of furniture. We'll add three coats using a rag ball and let it dry.

7 We tape off the edges of the tabletop with masking tape to protect the frame of visible wood that we don't want to paint.

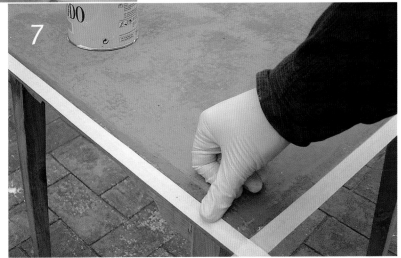

8 We'll paint a coat of water-based primer onto the center of the tabletop. We let it dry, sand, and then apply more coats until we have an even and smooth coat that we'll use as the base for our stamps.

9   Now it's time for our decorative finish. We pick out three colors for the background and start adding several large spots of color to the white background. We first paint on our burgundy colors that will contrast with the green tones.

10   Next, we paint on some dark green. We are covering large, irregularly shaped areas.

11   We finish off with our light green, filling in any spots that might still have white peeking through.

12 Once the first coat is dry, we'll add a second coat of each color. The different-colored background should be opaque.

13 While we let the background dry, we'll get our stamps ready by cutting out shapes from our foams and sponges. We'll also use a case, a cord, bubble wrap, textured cork, etc.

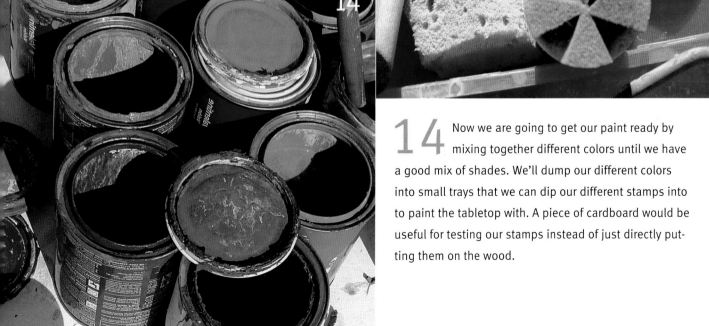

14 Now we are going to get our paint ready by mixing together different colors until we have a good mix of shades. We'll dump our different colors into small trays that we can dip our different stamps into to paint the tabletop with. A piece of cardboard would be useful for testing our stamps instead of just directly putting them on the wood.

15 We start stamping the tabletop with our wider stamps, such as the bubble wrap and cork. We let the first batch dry before we add any more. Now we'll move along with some of our small shapes. We will try not to completely fill up the tabletop with stamps. We want to be able to appreciate the shapes without going overboard. It's a good idea not to overload our stamps with paint to avoid messing up the images, which we can avoid by shaking the stamps off into our paint trays.

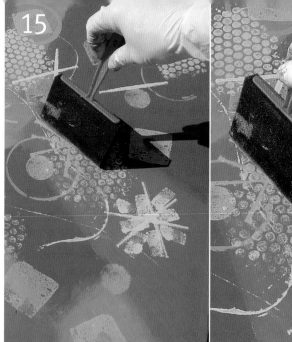

16 We take off the masking tape and scratch off any bits of primer or paint that might have made their way under the tape when we were painting.

17 Finally, we'll add a couple of coats of matte polyurethane varnish.

A Virtual Tablecloth

We bought this pine table at a great price at a big commercial storage site. We took it because of its simple design and the many possible decorations we could add to it. Plus, since it was new, we won't have to fix or restore it.

Idea

Our idea here is to use the wood as a background, protecting it and using transparent dyes to create motifs.

We will reinterpret a linear design inspired by traditional tablecloths and create our own unique finish.

Technique

The use of transparent and colorful paint is the secret to this delicate finish. The transparency will let the different colors work through each other, allowing every coat to be visible. We'll combine three colors: white, light pink, and fuchsia.

Assessment

Since we are dealing with natural wood, it will be essential to protect it with a sealer and varnish.

Materials

Preparing:
- Transparent wood sealer
- Rag ball
- Fine- and medium-grit sandpaper or sander
- Clean rag
- Gloves

Decorating:
- Pencil and ruler
- Masking tape
- Matte or satin water-based varnish
- Pink and white dye
- Containers for mixing paint
- Fine- and medium-sized decorating brushes
- Foam roller

Before starting . . .

The trick

The success of this method will depend on an even coat of varnish mixed with dye applied before the paint. We must meticulously prepare the mixture so we can avoid any lumps and achieve an appropriate transparent tone and texture.

We advise drawing up a sketch beforehand so you can visualize the design and placement of the lines.

Step by step

1 We start by sanding down the entire surface of natural wood with an electric sander or medium-grit sanding sponge. The tabletop should be quite soft to the touch. We clean off all the dust with a clean towel and then use a rag ball to apply a couple coats of wood sealer. Let it dry.

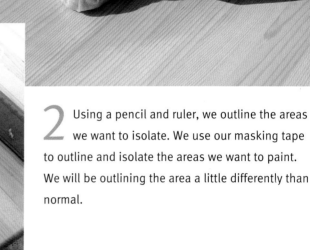

2 Using a pencil and ruler, we outline the areas we want to isolate. We use our masking tape to outline and isolate the areas we want to paint. We will be outlining the area a little differently than normal.

3 The masking tape should be placed underneath the supports for the tabletop, since the decoration should look like a tablecloth that is flowing over the edge.

4 We erase our pencil markings from the area we will be painting. Using a rag, we clean the leftover bits of glue and dust off the wood.

5 Now we get our dye ready. In one cup, we put the light pink; in another, the white (about one spoonful each).

6 We add varnish little by little to each dye until we have a dense but smooth mixture. We'll add a little more varnish now until we arrive at a creamy consistency. If we need to, we can add a little bit of water to smooth the texture of the mixture. To make sure we have the right tone, it's a good idea to try the colors on a piece of wood before painting the actual table.

Remember that when we're working with masking tape, it's best not to use very watery paint since they can slip under the tape, jeopardizing our end results.

7 In a third cup, we mix equal parts of pink and white to create an intermediate color.

8 Following our sketch, we start painting our lines with a paintbrush, painting first in the direction of the line and then perpendicular to it to erase any brush strokes in the paint. We paint all the lines using our three colors.

It was very common for old colorful tablecloths to be transparent.

9 Now we'll add a second and third coat, being consistent with our brush strokes and letting the paint dry in between each coat.

10 Now we carefully remove the masking tape and let everything dry before we start with our crosswise lines. Don't forget to cover the cups of paint and soak the paintbrushes in water.

11 We repeat step 2 and outline our crosswise lines using a pencil.

12 Once again, we'll place our masking tape along our new lines and erase any pencil marks.

13 Using the same colors, we'll apply a first coat, following our sketched outline.

14 Now we add another couple of coats, keeping our lines straight and transparent. We carefully remove the masking tape and let it all dry for a few hours.

15 To finish up, we'll protect the decorative finish with two coats of satin water-based varnish applied with a paint roller.

An Inspired Spice Rack

Imagine the number of containers and packaging that could be turned into unique objects or useful pieces of furniture. In this particular case, we are dealing with a wood box/case that used to have a collection of wine bottles. When we stand it on end, the box becomes a small closet with its compartments turning into convenient shelves.

Idea

We want to transform this wine box/case into a small spice rack for the kitchen. All we have to do is rearrange the lower shelves and stabilize them. They'll be perfect.

Technique

For the decorative finish, we'll play with some matte and satin tones. The satin will be our protective layer of orange plastic paint and the matte will form a coat of black oil-based paint. The satin varnish will serve to protect from blotches, will be easy to clean, and suitably hygienic.

We'll also use some cut out shapes in between our coats of color to make some great designs.

Assessment

The box is made of dense pinewood and the shelves are plywood. The iron fittings work perfectly but some of the joints are not attached well. We should reinforce the shelves as well as change the inner configuration so we can place taller jars. With the help of a jigsaw, we'll cut different-sized wooden slats (taking measurements straight from the case).

To reinforce the shelves, we'll place several small slats across the back of each panel (you'll see how this is done in step 12). We'll also use some slats to reinforce the door.

Before starting . . .

The trick

This piece could be transformed into a very functional and durable tool. Using the existing features of the box, we will just rearrange some of the shelves and reinforce them to adapt to their new contents.

We suggest taking precise measurements and making sketches beforehand to simplify this process. The motif on the door will be done with some small covers made from masking tape.

Materials

Preparation:
- Contact cement
- Wood filler
- Trowel
- Sanding sponge and sandpaper, medium grit
- Electric sander

Transforming:
- Jigsaw or handsaw
- Masking tape

- Hammer
- Clean rags
- Ruler and pencil
- Wooden slats

Decoration:
- White primer
- Orange (tangerine) plastic matte paint

- Medium paintbrush
- Small paint roller and tray
- Satin oil-based varnish
- Black matte oil-based paint (or black chalkboard paint)
- Turpentine or solvent

Step by step

1 We'll start by taking off the screwed in iron fittings and the shelves that can be easily pulled out.

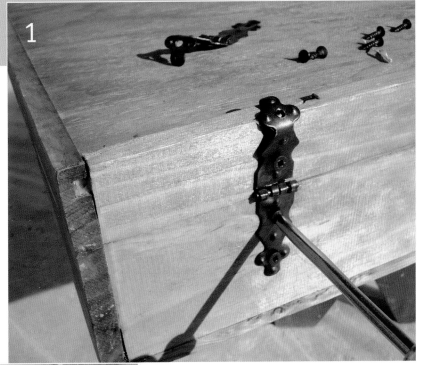

2 We'll fill the cracks, chips, and knots we find along the surface of the wood. We'll do the same thing to the imperfection on the top of the lid.

3 We let the filler dry and sand it down with our electric sander and/or sanding sponge, being careful not to damage the filler too much while evening out the surface. We repeat the process of adding filler if needed.

The base coat is very important for achieving a high quality finish. The surface of the wood needs to be smooth and even.

4 We shake off the case and clean up any dust with a damp rag.

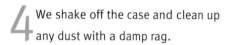

5 We will also sand the shelves so they have a smooth surface and so that their visible edges are also evened out. We clean up the dust.

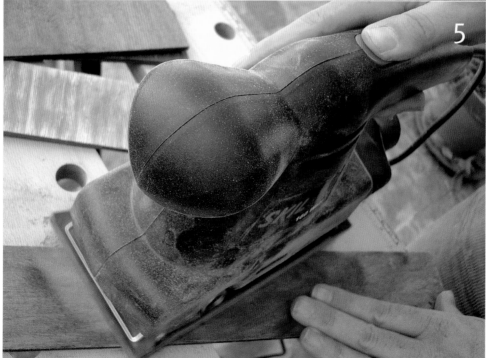

6 Now we'll rearrange the inside dividers to create some new shelves that are better suited for a spice rack. We can use the dividers that came with the rack to switch up the configuration. We'll mark on the back of the case what our new configuration for the shelves will be.

We'll also use a pencil to mark the cuts we'll be doing to the shelves, using a triangle to make sure the angles are correct and taking measurements straight from the box itself. We use a jigsaw to cut out the pieces.

7 We'll make a fitting between the two crosswise boards by carving a notch in the middle where they will be able to fit into each other, forming a cross. The vertical part will make the shelves more sturdy.

8 In the back of the box, we outline the places that we'll be putting contact cement using masking tape (on either side of the pencil markings). This way, we'll avoid leaving buildups of cement that are hard to remove and will damage our end product.

9 Using a trowel, we spread cement on the areas we've isolated in the back of the box and on the edges of the shelves that will be glued in.

10 We remove the masking tape and let the cement dry for fifteen to thirty minutes.

11 We'll fit the shelves in place, lining them up against the cement and applying pressure by tapping on them so we know there is solid contact where we put cement. Remember that the contact cement is too hard to be touched up, so this must be done right the first time.

12 We reinforce the shelves by placing small slats along the edges. The slats will also serve as a border that will keep jars from falling off. We secure the slats with white glue and apply pressure. We are also going to glue some slats to the inside of the door as reinforcement. We'll let it dry for twenty-four hours.

13 Now it's time for the decorative finish. We'll start with a coat of sealer over the entire case. After sanding and cleaning off the dust, we can apply more sealer anywhere that we didn't get well on the first pass. We let everything dry for a night.

14 We apply a coat of orange (tangerine) matte plastic paint that has been diluted a little over the entire case. We use a small brush to accurately apply paint to all the corners. The coats will dry quickly, so we can apply several in one day. We'll let it dry for a night.

15 We apply a couple of coats of satin varnish with a foam roller. We let it dry for a night.

16 Use masking tape to outline and isolate the areas we are going to paint in black.

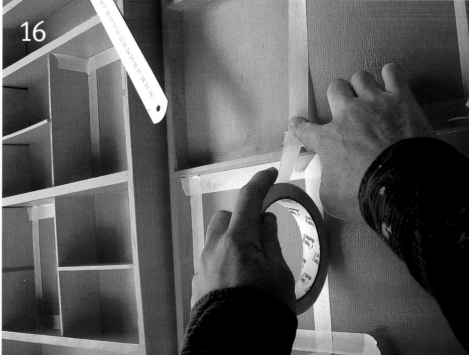

17 We will do the same thing to the part of the door that we are also going to paint with our decorative motif. Using our pencil, we outline the shape we want.

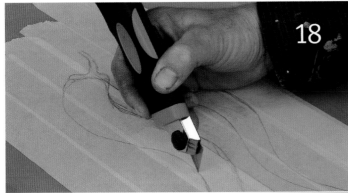

18 Using a utility knife, we cut out the silhouette of our shape, taking care to cut only the tape. That way, we will be able to preserve the shape we want with the color of the background.

19 Carefully take off the leftover bits of tape around the shape.

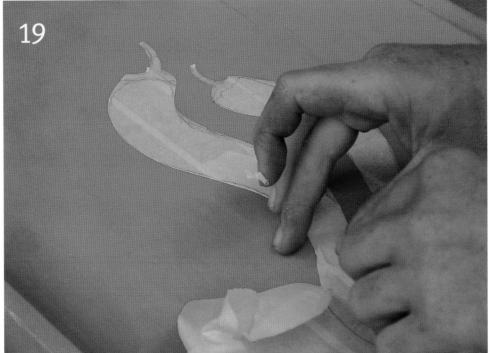

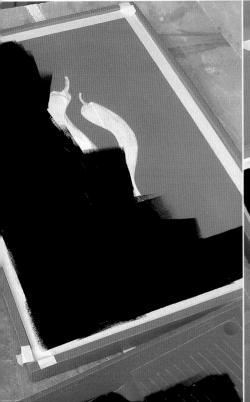

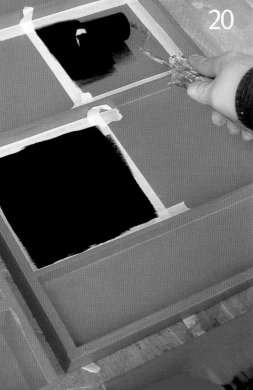

20 Using a roller, we apply our black matte oil-based paint (or chalkboard paint). Be careful not to accidentally paint the sides since the solvent we would have to use to clean up would damage the varnish coat or leave a stubborn black spot that we definitely don't want.

When the paint is completely dry, we remove all the masking tape and let everything dry.

21 Once the finish is dry, we place all the iron fittings back on and add a little handle to the door. We mark the spot where it will go and delicately drill some guide holes into the side of the door.

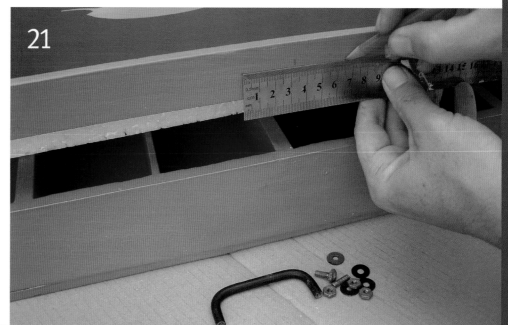

22 We place the handle against our guide holes and screw it in. We will also take this time to attach the pieces that will hold the rack onto the wall to the back upper half of the wood.

23 The final touch: on the inside of the door, we screw in some black-painted wooden clothes-pins that would be great for hanging small bags, envelopes, dry herbs, etc. We used an extra strong two-part glue for this.

Decoupage

Paper, with its different textures, colors, and motifs, is an excellent material that we can use for all kinds of unique finishes when we are refinishing our old furniture. This cheap material is easy to use, never goes out of style, and is the perfect ally for giving the furniture in your home a unique and imaginative touch. You could also use this technique to cover up imperfections or botched finishes.

Pop Table

This simple nightstand is not a terribly interesting piece of furniture, but there are certain small details that really attract us, such as the feet and the inside drawer. This is a pretty commonplace piece of furniture, often seen in apartments in the fifties, with a simple and somber appearance. The surfaces are smooth and easy to work with, which will make it a lot easier to give it a much more daring, original, and fun look.

Idea

We are going to completely change the look of this piece and give it a real fun touch. So, we decide to flood this piece with color, inspired by the bold and decorative styles of the eighteenth century, and adding a pop twist. To achieve the look we want, we'll use bright gift wrap, which can be bought in a number of colors and patterns.

Technique

The wrapping technique will let us create a finish using delicate patterns that will completely transform the piece. The difficulty in applying glue to the wrapping paper is getting a smooth, even surface without bubbles or buildups.

Before starting . . .

Assessment

The structure of this piece of furniture is in good shape, if a little damaged by woodworm, especially in the unvarnished areas. The entire piece is also covered in a thin coat of dark, ancient varnish that is chipping in places. The furniture is made of wood boards mounted atop a structure made of dense wood slats. The board on the top is raised up and cracked in certain areas.

Materials

Stripping:
▸ Paint scraper

Fixing:
▸ Woodworm killer or petroleum
▸ Wood filler
▸ Trowel
▸ Paint brush
▸ Syringe
▸ Sanding sponge and sandpaper

Preparing:
▸ Water-based white sealer

Finish:
▸ Paintbrush and/or rolling pin
▸ White glue
▸ Water
▸ Gift wrap
▸ Scissors
▸ Water-based varnish
▸ Foam roller

Step by step

1   We start by scraping down the entire
    surface of the piece of furniture to
take off the varnish coat.

2   We apply woodworm killer onto the
    entire nightstand. Using a syringe,
we will also fill the holes left behind by the
xylophagous insects.

3   Once dry, we fill the holes and the chips with a
    neutrally colored wood filler (cream). In one of the
corners, the sheet of wood has been quite damaged, so we
decide to take it off and completely remake it with filler. Let
it dry.

4   We sand down the entire piece of furniture with
    a sanding sponge, evening out all the filled
areas and smoothing down the surfaces.

5 We cover the entire nightstand with a coat of white, water-based sealer, sanding in between coats with very fine-grit sandpaper to make sure everything is nice and smooth. We will let it dry overnight.

6 Next, we'll cut out strips of paper or other shapes, depending on the desired pattern and how we want to apply the paper. By using smaller pieces of paper, the application process will be easier.

7 In a tin, we mix white glue with a bit of water (two parts glue to one part water) until the glue is nice and creamy and more easily applied. By using a thinner coat, we'll be left with a transparent film that we'll be able to see through after it dries. To begin, we apply glue to the back of the strips of paper, working on top of a flat, clean, and dry surface. We let the paper soak in the glue and swell a bit, but not for so long that the glue dries.

8 Now we are going to add glue to the wood so we can make sure the paper sticks evenly and completely.

9 Making sure the patterns and shapes match up, we take the strips of paper and carefully place them on the surface we have applied glue to.

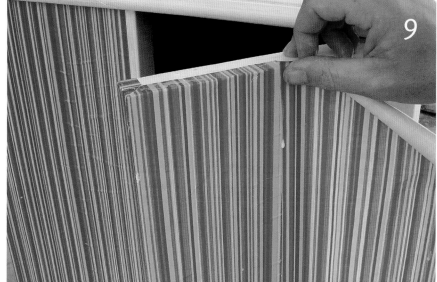

10 Using a dry towel, we press down on the paper, starting from the center and moving towards the edges to remove bubbles and smooth wrinkles. It's important to do this gently so we don't tear the paper.

11 Now we move on to the corners and edges, adding the paper using the same method as before. We press down with our fingers so that the paper conforms to the wood. Normally, these parts should be done before the flat areas.

12 When you get to the corners of the edges, remember that this kind of paper only folds in one direction. The strip of paper should extend beyond the edge of the corner so that we can cut off the excess afterwards. Now we continue to the other edge, adding the paper the same way. Finally, we cut off all the excess paper along the outer edge of the piece of furniture.

13 Once everything is glued on, we let it all dry for a whole night. The next day, we cut off the extra bits around the hinges and give it a couple of final coats of undiluted satin or matte water-based varnish.

14 To finish, we screw on the handles, poking a clean hole through the paper beforehand where the screws will go to avoid ripping it later.

A Day at the Market

We are more than used to seeing crates like these in shops and markets, but we've never really paid them any attention. Well, get ready, because in this book we really do use everything we can.

Idea

These boxes are fairly fragile and delicate. They are very thin and easily broken. Because of this, we will focus on their structure above all. We want to have a very nice finish that is resistant enough to stand the test of time.

Technique

To breathe new life into these old crates, we'll give them a "second skin" that will reinforce the wood and provide a striking finish. For this project, we've chosen to glue the wood and apply a decoupage of decorative napkins.

The multiple layers of absorbent paper will satisfy both our needs for this project: protection and decoration. The white glue absorbed into the paper will harden and reinforce the structure when it dries, creating a sturdy, multi-colored shell. We must always keep in mind, of course, that working with paper requires a certain amount of patience and care because we don't want to ruin our finish.

Materials

Decorating:
▸ White glue
▸ Paint brush
▸ Sets of decorative napkins
▸ Scissors
▸ Rags
▸ Hair dryer (optional)

Assessment

Market crates like these tend to have hectic lives, subjected to the clattering of trucks, stains from fruits, vegetable matter, dirt, water, etc. For this reason, we want to be careful when choosing a few crates for our project. These are usually made from thin sheets of pinewood, held together with staples (some more sturdy than others). Keep in mind that this type of wood is very delicate and hard to repair when it breaks. So, we want to pick out boxes that are in good shape, clean, and without splinters or chips that will make them harder to move and restore.

Before starting . . .

Step by step

1 We start by cleaning the boxes and taking off the rests of the stickers, logos, or bits of netting that are stuck or stapled to the boxes. If the staples are iron, we can avoid them rusting by applying a coat of primer. Once they are clean, we'll prepare a mixture of white glue and water (a 3:2 mix). We start applying the glue and water mixture with a paintbrush over parts of the boxes that will be covered with the napkins.

2 We stretch the napkins over the surface we've soaked with glue. We use our hands or a dry towel to gently smooth out the paper to get rid of any bubbles or wrinkles.

The trick

The soaked napkins are very fragile and delicate while they dry, so it's better not to touch the finish until everything is nice and dry. For this reason, we want to work on the boxes in stages, letting one side dry before we start on the next.

We would also advise working with several boxes at the same time to cut down on drying time and speed up the whole project. We could also use the hair dryer or place the boxes near a radiator to quicken the process.

3 Using a paintbrush, we'll soak the napkin with diluted glue. This will allow the paper to start picking up some resistance.

4 We will continue cutting out pieces and gluing the bare areas.

5   We completely cover the handles on the sides with more paper. We wait for the paper to dry a bit and start cutting out the center pieces in such a way that we can glue the paper around the edge. Then, we will cover the other side, using the same method for the holes as before.

6   We do the same to the bottom of the box. Once we've completely covered the bottom of the inside, we let it all dry for a little bit. We spin the box around, cut out the paper covering the gaps between the wood with a utility knife, and glue the flaps to the rim.

7 We cut out strips of napkin as wide as the wood boards we are working on. We glue the bare areas and finish covering them with paper. Let it dry.

8 We touch up any defects by gluing on patches and redoing any botched paper. Depending on how we want to use these boxes, we could apply a finishing coat of white glue or varnish (water or oil-based, preferably matte or satin).

Attractive Bathroom Cupboard

Formica furniture (made with melamine) became very popular during the seventies. It was affordable, practical, washable, and easily disassembled. But as the years went by, its look has gone out of style and many of the pieces have suffered moisture damage to their plywood, as well as their particleboard. We found this bathroom cupboard in a second-hand store, at a very affordable price. We were drawn by this piece's functional shape with shelves and mirror. We want to change its entire look and adapt it to a real bathroom.

Idea

We will completely change the look of this piece by painting the entire thing with a strong, brilliant, dynamic color somewhere between green and yellow: lime. On top, we'll apply some black-and-white copies of some illustrations found in a book of prints.

Technique
Two finishes:

Painting over the melamine. The smooth and impermeable surface that makes it hard to apply paint directly must be cleaned of any grease and then lightly sanded. Next, we'll cover it in a coat of gripping primer that will let us apply any decorative finish we want. A small foam roller would be the perfect tool for painting a surface as smooth and slick as the melamine.

Cut out and glued-on photocopies. Photocopying is a great way to scale up pictures and, above all, prints, since they are made using black lines that stand up well when enlarged. In this case, applying the decoupage is much simpler than trying to replicate a detailed drawing.

Assessment

The piece of furniture is in good shape. The melamine finish is chipping off at the corners, most like due to the stresses of traveling.

The trick

Melamine is a synthetic material that, until now, has been hard to get anything to stick to. But recently, there have been new, easy-to-use and useful primers on the market that will let us refinish this very seventies piece of furniture. We advise planning the work out beforehand to preview the placement and sizes of the motifs.

Before starting . . .

Materials

Cleaning:
- Solvent
- Rags

Fixing:
- Wood filler
- Medium-grit sandpaper
- Screwdriver

Preparation:
- Foam roller and paint tray
- White, water-based gripping primer
- Masking tape

Decoration:
- Lime-colored plastic paint
- Foam roller and paint tray
- Decorating brush
- Botanical encyclopedia prints or other scalable images
- Scalpel
- White glue and decorating brush
- Matte oil-based polyurethane varnish
- Foam roller for varnishing and a paint tray

Step by step

1 Before starting any work, we need to deeply clean this piece of furniture. To degrease it, we will wipe it down using a rag that we soaked in solvent.

2 Next, we'll fill all the chips in the corners with filler and sand it down after we have let it dry. This will even up the surfaces.

3 Now it's time to take apart the doors, the iron fittings, and the closing magnets.

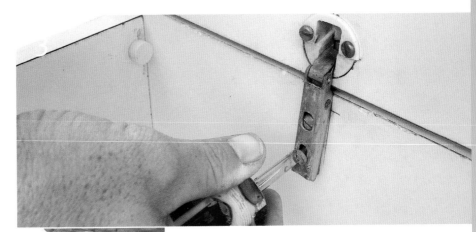

4 To avoid getting anything on the mirror, we'll outline and isolate it with masking tape. We organize all the pieces that we will be painting; for example, we can put the doors on top of sawhorses and the drawers on some newspaper.

5 In our paint tray, we get some primer ready and use our roller to apply a couple of coats to the entire piece of furniture. We don't want to forget any edges, corners (we can use our decorating brush), the inside of the doors, and bottom of the drawers. We'll try to get rid of any marks left by the roller as we go along. Our aim is to have the smoothest surface possible. This primer will dry pretty quickly, so the second coat can go on after just an hour. We will let it dry overnight before starting with the finishing coat.

6 Now it's time to apply the color. In a paint tray, we get our lime paint ready and, using a roller, add it to the entire cupboard. We will need to apply three consecutive coats, spreading them out thin to avoid drips our buildups (avoid pressing down too hard on the roller to make this easier). The coats should be applied in different directions to avoid leaving marks from the roller.

7 For the decoupage, we've picked out some black-and-white botanical prints. It is important that the picture is able to be enlarged and copied. In other words, the original needs to be of a good quality for the finish to look good. Before heading to the copy shop, we need to calculate how big our copies need to be so that they look good on the cupboard. For example, if the original drawing is 10 cm (about 4 in.) and we want to put it on a 50 cm (about 20 in.) surface, we'll need to increase its size by a factor of five. We recommend always asking for a manager. It doesn't matter if the enlarged image spans across several pages, the joining parts will be hidden in the decoupage.

8 Once we have the enlarged image, we cut it out carefully with a scalpel. Use your free hand to hold down the paper and the areas you are cutting to avoid any tears.

9 Now, we get our cupboard ready by figuring out the exact placement of the images. To do this, we can lightly mark with a pencil on the surface of the cupboard where we will place the images.

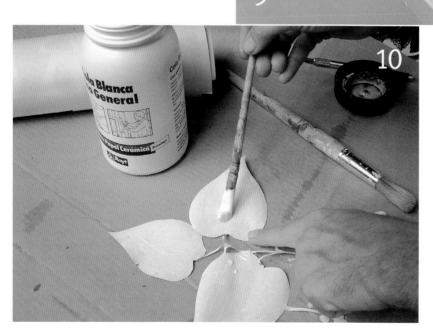

10 We apply white glue using a decorating brush to the back of the cutouts. We should use a clean, dry, and well-protected surface for applying our glue to the shapes without tearing them.

11 We place the cutouts on the marks we made in step 9.

12 We press it against the surface with our hand or a clean and dry rag, flattening the image at the center and moving outwards to get rid of any bubbles and to ensure it is all completely secured. We could keep going, gluing images to the interior and sides of the cupboard, by repeating the process. We can reapply glue to any edges or corners that have lifted up. We let everything dry overnight.

13 We will protect the finish with a couple of coats of varnish, applied using a paint roller, across the entire surface. We let everything dry.

14 Now we take off the masking tape and reattach the doors, the drawers, and all the iron fittings. We paint the decorative ring at the base of the handle black.

15 Finally, we replace the supports under the glass shelves with new ones.